THE SPIRITUAL EXERCISES
OF SAINT IGNATIUS

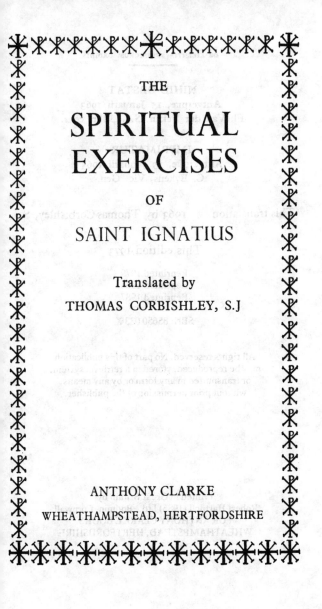

THE

SPIRITUAL
EXERCISES

OF

SAINT IGNATIUS

Translated by
THOMAS CORBISHLEY, S.J

ANTHONY CLARKE
WHEATHAMPSTEAD, HERTFORDSHIRE

DE LICENTIA SUPERIORUM ORDINIS

NIHIL OBSTAT
Antverpiæ, 15 Januarii 1963
Fl. Van der Veken, S.J., Libr. cens.

IMPRIMATUR
Antverpiæ, 15 Januarii 1963
C. Eykens, Vic. Gen.

This translation © 1963 by Thomas Corbishley, S.J.

This edition 1973

Reprinted 1979
Reprinted 1984
Reprinted 1987

SBN: 85650 033 X

Printed in Great Britain by
Robert Hartnoll (1985) Ltd., Bodmin, Cornwall
FOR ANTHONY CLARKE BOOKS
WHEATHAMPSTEAD, HERTFORDSHIRE

CONTENTS

Introduction 7
Notes 12
Premise 21

FUNDAMENTAL PRINCIPLE 22
A Daily Particular Examination of Conscience ... 22
A General Examination of Conscience 25
General Confession and Communion 28

FIRST WEEK:
First Exercise: The Triple Sin 30
Second Exercise: My own Sins 33
Third Exercise: A Repetition of the First and
  Second Exercises with Three Colloquies 34
Fourth Exercise: A Resumption of the Third
  Exercise 35
Fifth Exercise: A Meditation on Hell 35
Additional Practices 37
Notes 40

SECOND WEEK:
The King 42
First Day, First Contemplation: The Incarnation 45
Second Contemplation: The Nativity 47
Third Contemplation: Repetition 48
Fourth Contemplation: Repetition 48
Fifth Contemplation: An Application of the Sen-
  ses to the First and Second Contemplations .. 48
Notes 49
Second Day and Third Day 51
Introduction to an Examination of Different
  States of Life 51

Fourth Day: Meditation on Two Standards 52
Three Groups of Men 55
Fifth Day to Seventh Day 57
Eighth Day to Twelfth Day 58
Notes 58
Three Ways of Subjection 59
The Making of a Decision 60

THIRD WEEK:
First Contemplation: The Last Supper 67
Second Contemplation: The Garden 69
Notes 69
Second Day to Fifth Day 71
Sixth Day and Seventh Day 72
Rules for achieving Self-Control in the future
   with regard to Eating 73

FOURTH WEEK:
First Contemplation: The Resurrection 76
Notes 77

CONTEMPLATION FOR ACHIEVING LOVE 79

Three Ways of Praying 81
Events of the Life of our Lord Christ 86
Rules for distinguishing between Different Spi-
   ritual Influences 107
Almsgiving 115
About Scruples 118
The Mind of the Church 120

INTRODUCTION

It would be false to suggest that the Spiritual Exercises of St Ignatius were ever intended by their author to provide spiritual reading in the ordinarily accepted sense of that term; and he would probably have been a little surprised at the idea of putting the text into the hands of the faithful at large, without the control of an experienced director to advise on its use. In his opinion, the Spiritual Exercises were, as their name implies, not a subject for mere reading but a handbook for those engaged in the energetic activity of "making a retreat". What then is the justification for bringing out an edition intended to be widely available for individual devotional use?

Apart altogether from the fact that there are already in existence a number of editions and versions readily accessible to the general public, it cannot be denied that the situation in the Church today, in no small measure because of the work that he did, is very different from that which prevailed in the sixteenth century, at the time when the Exercises were first composed. In those days, the practice of making retreats was very restricted, whereas today many Catholics, from their school-days onwards, have become familiar with it. The growth in number of retreat houses, the widely-accepted custom of annual retreats (however brief) made by different and widely diverse groups, to say nothing of the undoubted fact that the ideas and the very framework of the Exercises have entered into much of the preaching of perhaps a majority of priests —all this means that the contents of St Ignatius's manual have become, at least in outline, widely known.

At the same time, there still clings to the book itself a certain element of mystery. Those who have merely heard some dramatic story of a change of heart effected by a retreat may be under the impression that the Exercises are an elaborate psychological mechanism, a cross between a course of spiritual Pelmanism and an alchemical formula. On a first acquaintance with the work itself, many experience a sense of disappointment. They cannot see what all the fuss is about. They thought to find a short-cut to sanctity and all they find is a collection of familiar theological ideas and hackneyed scriptural texts, side by side with naïve mediaeval imagery, a rather unsubtle psychology and what seems to them a regrettably reactionary attitude to authority.

It is, of course, true that the Exercises are very much a product of their age. If, at times, they seem to us moderns not merely dated but out-of-date, this may well be because they have done their work so well. Most of us must be familiar with the experience of reading some book in our youth which, at the time, seemed to open up new vistas of truth, unsuspected visions of glory, only to find that, when we return to it in later years, it seems to us very ordinary indeed, so that we cannot understand how we ever felt inspired as we did. The explanation, of course, lies in the fact that we are now what we are because of such past experiences. If the ideas in that book of our youth now seem to us quite commonplace, this is due to the effect of the book itself in having shaped our minds.

So it is possible that a mere reading of the text of the Exercises may evoke in us a combination of mild irritation, mild bewilderment and mild boredom. But, for all that, they are much more than an archaic survival, interesting to the historian or the scholar but without much significance to the ordinary man. The plain truth is that, in this book, we have a compendium of spirituality which is unique in the annals of Christian ascetic and spiritual literature. To the superficial reader it may seem to be lacking in depth and subtlety. But the experienced student of the work knows that it contains a surprising wealth of suggestion and inspiration.

This is why the Exercises are not to be *read* so much as *prayed*. A cursory reading is bound to lead to disappointment. But, treated as their author would have us treat them, as opportunities for developing our spiritual stamina and not just for satisfying our idle curiosity, they can continue to produce the effects which, for the last four hundred years, they have produced, to the lasting benefit of individual souls and of the Church of God.

Indeed it could well be argued that, although they were composed with a very different philosophical and theological situation in mind, their value today is not less but actually greater than it was in the sixteenth century. In those days, whatever divergences in theological outlook might prevail, the civilized world was essentially Christian and, still more, accepted a whole range of ideas which are being increasingly challenged and discarded. Not only the existence of God is being doubted; the fundamental human and social values are being questioned—man's freedom and moral responsibility, the reality of sin, the importance of certain essential virtues, the need to subordinate any and every kind of material and mechanical progress to man's spiritual welfare.

To this mentality the Exercises present a direct challenge. St Ignatius, heir of the Middle Ages rather than of the Renaissance, never for one moment doubted the reality and truth of the traditional Christian picture of man and his destiny. If we are to resist the erosion of our Christian and human values, we can hardly do better than to withdraw, however temporarily, from the sceptical climate that surrounds us and contemplate steadily the eternal verities as accepted and propounded by the author of the Exercises. If we can do this in retreat, so much the better. Even if we do make an annual retreat, it is well to be able to refresh our memories of that experience by a study of the text of St Ignatius's great manual.

But if we cannot, for one reason or another, retire into a retreat house, we shall do well to use the text of the Exercises as the subject-matter for our prayer. For far too many good Christians, "prayer" all too often is a matter of reciting set formularies, instead of really "raising mind and heart to God". Amongst other things, Ignatius helps us to learn to pray in a richer sense, and provides us with an immense variety of themes for prayer.

For all these reasons, then, there seems ample justification for making the text of the Exercises available as widely as possible, not alone to retreat-givers or those actually "in retreat", but to all who are concerned to deepen their appreciation of Christian truth and strengthen themselves in the living of a full Christian life.

In the present translation, as will be seen, a deliberate attempt has been made to find alternative renderings for many of the consecrated phrases of Christian ascetic writing. The simple fact is that most of these expressions have become so hackneyed that familiarity with them breeds, not indeed contempt, but certainly a dullness of appreciation. One minor, but not unimportant, reason why for so many people the whole affair of the "spiritual life" is suffused with boredom is because the traditional language is so faded and colourless. Certainly those who have had the experience of making retreats over many years know how the very text of the various meditations loses its edge by repetition, and how refreshing it can be to have St Ignatius's ideas presented with entire fidelity and yet with a novelty of language and illustration. There will, doubtless, be those who regard the familiar English of Fr Morris's text as somehow sacred; and these are likely to feel affronted at any change of expression.

Yet the present version, which has been made on the basis of the original Spanish, but with careful reference to renderings in different languages, claims to be an honest attempt to present St Ignatius's thought in language which will bring out his meaning more effectively and possibly more faithfully. The translation does not pretend to incorporate all the latest findings of Ignatian scholars, nor the notes seek to replace the still valuable work of Father Joseph Rickaby or Father Longridge. Their commentaries will be needed to supplement the necessarily limited comments of an edition which is meant to be primarily a simple presentation of a work of abiding significance for Christians both learned and unlearned.

NOTES

1. The name "Spiritual Exercises" means every form of examination of conscience, of meditation, contemplation, prayer (vocal and mental) and the spiritual activities mentioned later. Going for long or short walks and running are physical exercises; so we give the name of spiritual exercises to any process which makes the soul ready and able to rid itself of all irregular attachments, so that, once rid of them, it may look for and discover how God wills it to regulate its life to secure its salvation.

2. The person who gives another the method and outline for meditation or contemplation must faithfully recount the historical subject of such a contemplation or meditation, just running over the headings in a brief and summary explanation; the reason for this is that when the person making the contemplation is given the basic facts of the story and then goes over it and thinks about it for himself, any discovery he makes which sheds light on the story, or brings it home to him more, will give him greater delight and more benefit of soul. Such discoveries may be due to his own reflection or to the divine action, but they are better than if the giver of the exercises had gone into great detail and expounded at length the significance of the story. Nor does the soul's full satisfaction come

from wide knowledge so much as from the personal appreciation of and feeling for things.

3. In all the following spiritual exercises we make acts of the understanding in reasoning and acts of the will in being moved to action; we must be careful to note that, in those acts of the will in which we hold converse (in word or thought) with our Lord God or His Saints, greater reverence is required of us than when we are employing our reasoning faculties.

4. Four weeks are assigned to the following exercises, corresponding with their four divisions : first, reflection on and contemplation of sins; second, the life of Christ our Lord, up to and including Palm Sunday; third, the sufferings of Christ our Lord; fourth, the Resurrection and Ascension, with three ways of Praying, as an appendix. But these four weeks are not to be understood as each consisting of seven or eight days. In the first week some may be slower to find what they want, namely contrition and tears of sorrow for their sins, whilst some are more earnest, or more disturbed and tried by different spiritual influences: so sometimes the first week will have to be shortened, sometimes lengthened, and so with the following weeks, having in mind all the time what the given subject-matter is meant to effect. Still, the whole course should be completed in approximately thirty days.

5. The retreatant will benefit greatly if he starts with a largehearted generosity towards his Creator and Lord, surrendering to Him his freedom of will, so that His Divine Majesty may make that use of his person and possessions which is in accordance with His most holy will.

6. When the retreat-giver sees that the retreatant is not spiritually affected in any way, experiencing neither spiritual comfort nor distress nor being worked upon by different spiritual influences, he should question him closely about his performance of the exercises, whether he is doing them at the fixed times and in what way, whether, too, he is observing the Additional Practices carefully. He should investigate these matters in detail. ["Comfort" and "distress" are treated in §§ 316-324: the Additional Practices are given in §§ 73-85.]

7. If the retreat-giver sees that the retreatant is undergoing distress and temptation, he must not be harsh or severe but kind and considerate, encouraging and strengthening him for what is ahead, exposing the tricks of the enemy of mankind, reassuring him and doing all he can to put him into a suitable frame of mind for the comfort in store.

8. Judging from the retreatant's need, arising either from his distress and the enemy's tricks or from his experience of comfort, the retreat-giver may explain the rules, given in the first and second weeks, by which different spiritual influences may be distinguished.

9. Whilst the retreatant is going through the first-week exercises he may, if he has had little spiritual experience, be subjected to certain crude and obvious temptations; for example, he may manifest an awareness of certain obstacles to progress in the service of our Lord God, such as the thought of hardships, feeling ashamed, wondering what people will think about him, etc.; in this case the retreat-giver must be careful not to talk to him about the second-week rules for discriminating between different spiritual influence;

the first-week rules will help him, but the second-week rules will do him just as much harm, as they contain matter which is too subtle and too advanced for him.

10. When the retreat-giver realizes that the retreatant is being attacked by some temptation which comes in the form of some spurious good, it will be appropriate to tell him about the above-mentioned second-week rules: it usually happens that man's enemy tempts him by some spurious good when the retreatant is engaged in the way of enlightenment, corresponding to the second-week exercises; it happens less in the way of purification, corresponding to the first week.

11. It is a good thing for the retreatant in the first week not to know anything about what he will be doing in the second week: he should struggle in the first to get what he is looking for, as though he had no hope of getting anything in the second.

12. The retreat-giver should make it clear to the retreatant that he must spend an hour on each of the five exercises or contemplations to be made every day, so that he should find satisfaction of mind in the thought that he has remained a full hour, or even a little longer, in a given exercise; the enemy is in the habit of getting the hour of contemplation, meditation or prayer cut down.

13. Again it should be noticed that, whilst it is easy and pleasant to complete the full hour of contemplation in time of comfort, in time of distress it is very hard to finish it. So, in order to counter the distress and overcome the temptation, the retreatant must always go on a little longer than the full hour.

In this way he will get used not only to resisting the enemy but to routing him completely.

14. If the retreat-giver finds that the retreatant enjoys comfort and great fervour in the exercises, he should warn him against making any promise or vow, imprudently and hastily; all the more so if he recognizes in him an unstable temperament. True as it may be that one is justified in prompting another to enter religion, which implies taking the vows of obedience, poverty and chastity, true as it may be that a good deed performed under a vow carries with it more merit than one not so performed, yet the retreatant's peculiar condition must be borne in mind, as well as what helps or hindrances he may encounter in the fulfilment of any undertaking he may give.

15. It is not for the retreat-giver to turn the retreatant's thoughts to poverty or to the promise of any such thing rather than to the opposite, nor to one state or way of life rather than to another: outside the time of retreat we may properly and meritoriously induce those who, in all probability, have the necessary disposition to choose continence, virginity, religious life or any kind of evangelical perfection; but in the course of these spiritual exercises, it is more appropriate that, in the search for the divine will, the Creator and Lord should be left to deal Himself with the soul that belongs to Him, receiving it into His love and to a life of praise, fitting it for that form of service which will be best for it in the time to come. The retreat-giver, therefore, must not tend or incline to either side, but remain in perfect equilibrium, allowing the Creator to deal directly with His creature and the creature with his Creator and Lord.

16. For this same reason, namely, to allow the Creator to deal more surely with His creature, if it should happen that this person is improperly influenced and inclined in one direction, it is most fitting that he should use all his strength to strive towards the opposite of that which is the object of his improper desire. For instance, if he is on the look-out for and is anxious to hold some position or living, not for the honour and glory of our Lord God, or for the spiritual benefit of souls, but for his own temporal advantage and interest, he should turn his ambitions in the opposite direction: in his prayers and other spiritual exercises he should beg and plead with our Lord God for the contrary; he should, that is, insist that he does not want that position or living or anything else unless His Divine Majesty regulate his desire and change his former attitude. Thus his motive for holding the one or the other shall be solely the service, honour and glory of His Divine Majesty.

17. The retreat-giver, without wishing to pry into or know about the thoughts and sins personal to the retreatant, will be greatly helped if he is given precise information about the promptings and suggestions arising from different spiritual influences; for it is in accordance with the retreatant's progress that the retreat-giver will be able to propose suitable spiritual exercises, adapted to the needs of a soul thus affected.

18. Spiritual exercises must be adapted to the nature of those who wish to undergo them, suited, that is, to their age, education or ability: otherwise an unintelligent or simple-minded person may find some things beyond his capacity and therefore ineffective. Again, each should be given whatever is proper to what he has in mind, so that he may get help and benefit. For example, if the sort of help a man wants is to be put on the right path and to find some peace of mind, he might be given the particular examination of conscience [§§ 24-31] followed by the general examination [§§ 32-43]. Besides this, for half-an-hour every morning he should practise the way of praying about the commandments, the deadly sins, etc. [§§ 238-248]. He should be advised to confess his sins every week and, if possible, to receive Holy Communion every fortnight, or, better still, every week, if he is so inclined. This sort of retreat is better suited to the less intelligent or the uneducated, who should have explained to them the individual Commandments, the deadly sins, the commandments of the Church, the five senses and the works of mercy.

In the same way, if the retreat-giver realizes that the retreatant is not a strong character or is of limited ability, in whose case no great benefit is to be expected, it is better to give him some of the less demanding exercises, ending with confession; he can then be given some forms of examination of conscience, with instructions to go to confession more frequently. This will help him to retain such benefit as he has acquired. He should not go on to the matter of the Decision, nor to any other exercises after the first week. This is particularly important where there are others who could derive more benefit. There is not time for everything.

19. In the case of a man of education or ability, occupied with public affairs or essential business, if he can spend an hour and a half a day on the exercises, he should be given a homily on the purpose of man's

creation: in the same way, he can be given the particular examination for half-an-hour and then the general examination and the way of going to confession and receiving Holy Communion. Every morning for three days he should make the meditation on the first, second and third sins [§§ 45-54]. For three more days, at the same time, the meditation on the tale of his own sins [§§ 55-61], and for three days after that, at the same time, he must do the meditation on the punishments appropriate to sins [§§ 65-71], being given along with all three meditations the ten Additional Practices [§§ 73-85]. The same treatment should be kept for the events of our Lord's life, as is fully described in the exercises below.

20. If a man is less busy and is anxious to profit in every possible way, he should be given all the spiritual exercises in the order given below. He will normally profit more the more he withdraws from the society of all his friends and acquaintances, and from every temporal preoccupation, for instance, by leaving the house he lives in and taking another house or room to stay in, with as much privacy as possible. He will thus be able to go every day to Mass and Vespers, with no danger of interference from his own circle. This isolation will have, amongst others, three chief advantages:

(1) When a man cuts himself off from a host of friends and acquaintances and also from a mass of irregular business, to serve and praise our Lord God, he obtains no small merit in the eyes of His Divine Majesty.

(2) By remaining alone in this way and undistracted by many distracting concerns, he can direct his entire

attention to one purpose, that is to the service of his Creator and to his soul's advantage; he now devotes his talents with greater freedom to a concentrated search for that which he so ardently desires.

(3) The more our soul finds itself in perfect solitude, the fitter does it become to approach and reach up to its Creator and Lord; and the closer it gets to Him, the more disposed does it become to receive favours and gifts from His supreme divine goodness.

21. *SPIRITUAL EXERCISES*

FOR THE OVERCOMING OF SELF AND THE REGULATION OF ONE'S LIFE ON THE BASIS OF A DECISION ARRIVED AT WITHOUT ANY UNREGULATED MOTIVE

PREMISE

22. So that both the retreat-giver and the retreatant may get help and benefit, it is to be premised that every good Christian will be more inclined to put a good construction on another's statement than to fault it. If he is unable to find a good interpretation, he should ask what he means. If his meaning is unorthodox, the other should put him right, in a spirit of love. If this is not enough, let him use all the means proper to get the proposition rightly interpreted.

23. Man has been created to praise, reverence and serve our Lord God, thereby saving his soul.

Everything else on earth has been created for man's sake, to help him to achieve the purpose for which he has been created.

So it follows that man has to use them as far as they help and abstain from them where they hinder his purpose.

Therefore we need to train ourselves to be impartial in our attitude towards all created reality, provided we are at liberty to do so, that is to say it is not forbidden. So that, as far as we are concerned, we do not set our hearts on good health as against bad health, prosperity as against poverty, a good reputation as against a bad one, a long life as against a short one, and so on.

The one thing we desire, the one thing we choose is what is more likely to achieve the purpose of our creating.

A DAILY PARTICULAR EXAMINATION OF CONSCIENCE

INVOLVING THREE OCCASIONS AND A TWICE-REPEATED SELF-EXAMINATION

24. The first occasion is the moment of getting up in the morning. One should then resolve to watch carefully so as not to commit the particular sin or fault which one has decided to correct.

25. The second is after the midday meal, when one asks of our Lord God what one wants, the grace to recall how often one has fallen into that particular sin or fault and to amend for the future. So the first examination is made by exacting from one's conscience an account dealing with the particular fault it is proposed to correct, running over each hour or period of time, beginning from the moment of getting up until this present examination. An entry is made on the first line of the double line G [*see* p. 24], consisting of as many dots as there have been lapses into the particular sin or fault; then a fresh resolution is made to do better until the next examination is made.

26. The third occasion is after supper, when the second examination is made, going in the same way over the hours, beginning from the first examination until this second one and entering on the second line of the figure G as many dots as there have been lapses into the particular sin or fault.

27. Four additional practices are here given, for the quicker eradication of that particular sin or fault.

(1) Every time one falls into that particular sin or fault, the hand is laid on the breast in token of sorrow for the fall. This can be done even in company without its being noticed.

28. (2) As the first line of the figure G represents the first examination and the second one the second, it can be seen at night whether there has been any improvement between the two lines, i.e. between the two examinations.

29. (3) The second day should be compared with the first, that is, the two examinations of the present

day with the previous day's, so as to see whether there
has been any improvement from one day to the next.

30. (4) One week should be compared with the
previous one, to see if there has been any improvement
between the two.

31. *Note*. The first (capital) G in the following
diagram stands for Sunday, the second (small) g for
Monday, the third for Tuesday and so on.

G ....

   ....

g ....

   ....

g ....

   ....

g ....

   ....

g ....

   ....

g ....

   ....

g ....

   ....

A GENERAL EXAMINATION
OF CONSCIENCE

FOR SELF-PURIFICATION AND FOR MAKING A BETTER
CONFESSION

32. I assume that my thoughts are of three sorts, one my own, arising of my own free choice, the other two coming from outside, one from the good spirit, the other from the bad spirit.

THOUGHT

33. There are two ways of gaining merit from an evil thought which comes from outside me. For example, the thought occurs to me to commit a mortal sin, I resist it promptly and it is completely defeated.

34. The second way is when the same thought of committing a mortal sin occurs to me, and, though I resist it, it recurs again and again: I go on resisting until it is finally defeated. This second way gains more merit than the first.

35. A venial sin is committed when the same thought of sinning mortally occurs to me, and I listen to it, dwelling on it for some time or experiencing some sensual pleasure or showing some negligence in repelling it.

36. There are two ways of committing mortal sin. The first is when a man consents to the evil thought, with the idea of putting his consent into immediate effect, or intending so to act if he could.

37. The second way of sinning mortally is actually performing the sinful act. This is graver than the former sin for three reasons: *(a)* because more time is involved, *(b)* because of the greater intensity of consent, *(c)* because of the greater harm done to both parties.

38. No one may swear, either by the Creator or by a creature, unless truth, necessity and reverence all enter in. By necessity I mean not the swearing to any truth at all, but only when it is of some importance for the good of soul or body or for one's material advantage. By reverence I mean the attitude of a man who, calling on his Creator and Lord, duly bears in mind the honour and respect owing to Him.

39. It is to be noted that whilst an unnecessary oath is more sinful when we swear by the Creator than by a creature, yet it is more difficult to swear fittingly—that is with truth, necessity and reverence— by a creature than by the Creator, for these three reasons:

(1) When we decide to call some creature to witness an oath, the very fact that we are swearing by a creature makes us less careful and scrupulous about telling the truth, or about the necessity of such affirmation, than when we choose to call on the name of the Lord and Creator of the universe.

(2) When we swear by the creature it is harder to show reverence and respect for the Creator than when we actually call upon the Creator and Lord Himself to witness our oath: for the very decision to invoke the name of our Lord God involves more reverence and respect than choosing to name a created object. Hence, those who are perfect may more easily be allowed to swear by the creature than those who are less perfect.

Those who are perfect, through constant reflection and because of the illumination of their minds, are more capable of realizing, meditating on and contemplating the fact of God's being in every creature by essence, presence and power. So, when swearing by a creature, they are more able and more prepared to show respect and reverence to the Creator than those who are less perfect.

(3) Through constant swearing by creatures there is more danger of idolatry on the part of those who are imperfect than of those who are perfect.

40. "Do not speak a thoughtless word" means, I take it, that what I am saying is no good either to myself or anyone else, nor is it intended to be. So it is never thoughtless to say what does good or is at least meant to be of advantage either to one's soul or body or estate, or to some one else's. Sometimes, even to speak of matters that do not belong to one's state of life is not thoughtless speaking, as when a religious speaks of wars or business. In all speech, there is merit in what is directed to a good purpose, sin in what is not so directed, and in thoughtless words.

41. Nothing should be said to take away another's character or for mere gossip. If I disclose a mortal sin not publicly known, I commit a mortal sin: if a venial sin, I commit a venial sin; if a fault, I show my own fault. Granted a right intention, there are two cases in which I may speak of another's sin or fault: *(a)* when the sin is public, as in the case of a known prostitute or of a sentence passed in open court or of some widespread fallacy affecting the minds of those I have to deal with; *(b)* when a sin not generally known is disclosed to one who may be able to help the sinner to overcome it, so long as there are good reasons for thinking that he may be helpful.

ACTION

42. Taking as our subject-matter the Ten Commandments, the Commandments of the Church and practices approved by Superiors, any action contrary to one of these divisions is a greater or smaller sin according to the gravity of the matter. By practices approved of by Superiors I mean such things as *bullæ cruciatæ* and other indulgences, such as those granted to the faithful who have been to confession and communion "for the peace of the Church". For it is no light sin to be the cause of others acting contrary to such approved practices or to act so oneself.

METHOD OF MAKING THE GENERAL EXAMINATION OF CONSCIENCE IN FIVE STAGES

43. (1) Give thanks to our Lord God for favours received.

(2) Ask for grace to know and to root out your sins.

(3) Demand of your conscience an hourly or periodic account, beginning with the moment of getting up until this examination, first as to thoughts, then words and then actions, in the way described in the Particular Examination.

(4) Ask pardon of our Lord God for these faults.

(5) Resolve, with the grace of God, to do better. An *Our Father*.

GENERAL CONFESSION AND HOLY COMMUNION

44. There are many advantages to be gained by spontaneously making a general confession during a retreat. These are the three chief ones:

(1) Whilst it is true that anyone who confesses every year is not bound to make a general confession, yet if he does he gains a greater benefit and more merit on account of the greater contrition he then experiences, as he thinks of the sins and iniquities of his whole life.

(2) During a retreat he has a more intimate appreciation of the wickedness of his sins than he had when he did not apply his mind in the same way to his spiritual life. By now getting greater knowledge of and sorrow for them, he will get more benefit and merit than he could have obtained previously.

(3) Having thus made a more effective confession and being in better dispositions, he will be more adequately prepared and in a worthier frame of mind for receiving the most holy Eucharist. Receiving it will not only help him to keep out of sin but will also enable him to retain that increased grace which he has obtained.

The best time for making the general confession is immediately after the first week.

FIRST WEEK

FIRST EXERCISE

THE TRIPLE SIN

45. A MEDITATION, using the three faculties, on the first, second and third sin: it contains a preparatory prayer and two preliminaries, followed by three headings and a colloquy.

46. *Preparatory prayer.* Ask our Lord God for the grace to direct my thoughts, activities and deeds to the service and praise of His Divine Majesty.

47. *First preliminary.* An imaginative representation of the place.
Note. For a visual contemplation or meditation, the picture is an imaginative representation of the physical place where the event to be contemplated occurs. By physical place I mean, e.g., a temple or mountain where Jesus Christ our Lord is, as demanded by the subject-matter. Where the subject-matter is not something visible, as in the present case of sins, the "picture" will be the idea, produced by an effort of the imagination, that my soul is a prisoner in this corruptible body and that my whole self, body and soul, is condemned to live amongst animals on this earth, like someone in a foreign land.

48. *Second preliminary.* I ask our Lord God for what I want. This prayer must be appropriate to the subject-matter. If I am contemplating the Resurrection, I will pray for a share in Christ's joy; if the

Passion, I will ask for suffering, grief and agony, in the company of Christ in agony.

Here my prayer will be that I may feel wholly ashamed of myself, thinking how often I have deserved eternal damnation for my frequent sins, whilst many have been lost for a single sin.

49. *Note.* Each contemplation or meditation is to be preceded by the preparatory prayer, which is never changed, and the two preliminaries mentioned above, which are to be varied with the subject-matter.

50. *First heading.* By an effort of my memory, I will recall the first sin, that of the angels; next, I will use my reason to think about it; then my will, striving to remember and think about all this in order to develop in myself a sense of utter shame, as I compare my numerous sins with the angels' one sin: that one sin brought them to Hell: how often have I deserved it for all my sins.

The memory's part is to recall how the angels were created in grace, but refused to make the most of their free-will in honouring and obeying their Creator and Lord: they fell victims to pride, and their state of grace was perverted to one of evil will, as they were plunged from Heaven into Hell.

Using my reason in the same way, I will think about all this in greater detail: by my will I try to evoke the proper sentiments.

51. *Second heading.* The same is to be done with the sin of Adam and Eve, and my three faculties should be applied. I will recall the long penance they had to do for that sin, the corruption which came upon mankind, with the result that so many went to Hell.

The second sin, then, that of our first parents, is to be thought of in memory in this way: Adam was created in the plain of Damascus and placed in the earthly paradise, Eve being formed from his rib. Though forbidden to eat of the tree of knowledge, they sinned by eating of it, were clothed in skins and cast out of paradise, to lead a life without that original innocence which they had lost; to the end they endured many hardships for their penance.

The understanding is to be used to think about all this in greater detail, and the will as described above.

52. *Third heading.* So with the third sin, the individual sin of anyone who has gone to Hell for one mortal sin; and many others, beyond counting, for fewer sins than I have committed. That is to say, I must apply to this third individual sin my memory, by recalling the gravity and monstrous nature of sin committed by man against his Creator and Lord: my understanding, by reflecting how eternal condemnation is a just retribution for a sinful act against infinite goodness: and finally my will, in the way already described.

53. *Colloquy.* Let me picture Christ our Lord hanging on the Cross before me, and speak to Him in this way: how has He, the Creator, come to be man? Knowing eternal life, how has He come to this temporal death, this death for my sins? Then, turning to myself, I will ask: What have I done for Christ? What am I doing for Christ? What must I do for Christ?

Seeing the state Christ is in, nailed to the Cross, let me dwell on such thoughts as present themselves.

54. The colloquy is really the kind of talk friends have with one another, or perhaps like the way a servant speaks to his master, asking for some kindness or apologising for some failure, or telling him about some matter of business and asking for his advice.

The colloquy ends with an *Our Father*.

SECOND EXERCISE

MY OWN SINS

55. A MEDITATION on my own sins. After the preparatory prayer and two preliminaries, it has five headings and a colloquy.

Prayer. The same preparatory prayer.

First preliminary. The same picture.

Second preliminary. Asking for what I want. Here a perfect sorrow and intense grief for my sins.

56. *First heading.* The story of my sins. I will recall to mind all the sins of my life, seeing them year by year or stage by stage. I can help myself in three ways: (1) seeing the locality or the house where I have lived; (2) thinking of my dealings with others; (3) the position I have held.

57. *Second heading.* I will think over my sins, looking at the ugliness and evil involved in any mortal sin, even if it were not forbidden.

58. *Third heading.* I will see what I am, making myself less and less important by these comparisons:

(1) What am I compared with the whole human race?

(2) What is the human race compared with the angels and saints in Heaven?

(3) What is the whole of creation compared with God? What, then, can I, by myself, be?

(4) Let me look at the foulness and ugliness of my body.

(5) Let me see myself as an ulcerous sore running with every horrible and disgusting poison.

59. *Fourth heading*. I will reflect on the nature and attributes of God against whom I have sinned, contrasting them with their opposites in me—His wisdom with my ignorance, His infinite power with my impotence, His justice with my wickedness, His goodness with my evil will.

60. *Fifth heading*. A shout of astonishment and profound love, as I think how every created thing has not refused to keep me alive. The angels, the sword of God's justice, have put up with me, protected me, prayed for me: the saints have gone on praying and interceding on my behalf: the sky, the sun, the moon, the stars, the natural elements, the fruits of the earth, birds, fish, the whole animal kingdom...; why has not the very earth opened to swallow me, creating new hells for my eternal torment?

61. *Colloquy*. I will end by telling of the mercy of God, thanking Him as I realize that He has given me life until this very moment, resolving that, with His grace, I will do better for the future. *Our Father*.

THIRD EXERCISE

A REPETITION OF THE FIRST AND SECOND EXERCISES, WITH THREE COLLOQUIES

62. AFTER the preparatory prayer and the two preliminaries, this will consist in a repetition of the first and second exercises. I should pay attention to and dwell specially on the points in which I experienced greater comfort or distress or some more marked spiritual effect.

63. Afterwards I will make these three colloquies:

First colloquy. With our Lady, that she may get for me from her Son the grace for three things: *(a)* a deep-felt consciousness of my sins and a profound disgust with them; *(b)* an appreciation of the irregularity of what I have done, so that, by hating that, I may lead a better and more regular life; *(c)* a knowledge of the world such that I may come to hate it and so give up all worldliness and folly. Then a *Hail Mary.*

Second colloquy. With the Son, asking Him to obtain the same graces from the Father, and ending with the *Anima Christi.*

Third colloquy. With the Father, that the same eternal Lord may grant my prayer. Then an *Our Father.*

FOURTH EXERCISE

A RESUMPTION OF THE THIRD EXERCISE JUST MADE

64. BY resumption I mean the process whereby the mind, without any digressing, recalls and considers carefully the matter of the previous contemplations, making the same three colloquies.

FIFTH EXERCISE

A MEDITATION ON HELL

65. AFTER the preparatory prayer and two preliminaries, it consists of five headings and a colloquy.

The preparatory prayer will be the usual one.

First preliminary. The picture. In this case it is a vivid portrayal in the imagination of the length, breadth and depth of Hell.

Second preliminary. Asking for what I want. Here it will be to obtain a deep-felt consciousness of the sufferings of those who are damned, so that, should my faults cause me to forget my love for the eternal Lord, at least the fear of these sufferings will help to keep me out of sin.

66. *First heading*. To see in imagination those enormous fires, and the souls, as it were, with bodies of fire.

67. *Second heading*. To hear in imagination the shrieks and groans and the blasphemous shouts against Christ our Lord and all the saints.

68. *Third heading*. To smell in imagination the fumes of sulphur and the stench of filth and corruption.

69. *Fourth heading*. To taste in imagination all the bitterness of tears and melancholy and a gnawing conscience.

70. *Fifth heading*. To feel in imagination the heat of the flames that play on and burn the souls.

71. *Colloquy*. Talk to Christ our Lord. Remember that some souls are in Hell because they did not believe He would come; others because, though they believed, they did not obey His commandments. They fall into three classes: (1) before His coming; (2) during His lifetime; (3) after His life on earth. Remembering this, I will thank Him that He has not allowed me to die and so to fall into one of these classes. I

will also thank Him for having shown me such
tender mercy all my life long until now; and will close
with an *Our Father*.

72. *Note.* The first exercise is to be made at midnight, the second immediately after getting up in the
morning, the third before or after Mass but before
the midday meal, the fourth at the time of Vespers
and the fifth an hour before supper.

This is roughly the time-table I presuppose in all
four weeks, in so far as the retreatant's age, physical
condition and temperament enable him to perform
all five exercises or only some of them.

ADDITIONAL PRACTICES

TO HELP THE RETREATANT TO MAKE THE EXERCISES BETTER
AND OBTAIN MORE EFFECTIVELY WHAT HE IS AIMING AT

73. (1) WHEN I have gone to bed and am just about
to fall asleep, I will turn my thoughts, for the length
of a *Hail Mary*, to the time I have to get up and what
I shall be getting up for, briefly running through the
exercise I have to make.

74. (2) On waking up, without letting my thoughts
wander at random, I will immediately think of the
subject I have to contemplate in the first exercise at
midnight. I will try to be ashamed of all my sins, using
illustrations; for example, I may think of a knight,
standing before his king and the whole court, utterly
ashamed at having greatly offended one from whom he
had received many gifts and acts of kindness. In the
same way, for the second exercise, I will see myself
as a great sinner, in chains, on my way to stand as a
prisoner before the Supreme Eternal Judge. I will

remember how prisoners, guilty of a capital crime, appear in fetters before an earthly judge. As I dress, I will have in mind thoughts like these and others appropriate to the subject-matter.

75. (3) Standing a few feet in front of the place where I am to make my contemplation, I will spend the length of an *Our Father* in the thought that our Lord God is watching me, and make an act of profound reverence.

76. (4) I will then begin my contemplation, which I will perform either on my knees or lying on the ground, prostrate or with my face upwards; or I may sit or stand, always thinking in terms of getting what I am looking for. Two things should be noted:

(a) If what I am looking for is granted to me when I am on my knees, I should not move on to another position; similarly, if it is granted when I am prostrate, and so on.

(b) I should dwell on the point which gives me what I am looking for, without being anxious to go on to the next stage before I am completely satisfied.

77. (5) After finishing the exercise, I will sit down or walk about for a quarter of an hour, and see how things have gone during the contemplation or meditation. If they have gone badly, I must look for the reason, and when I have found it I will be sorry, so as to do better in future; if things have gone well, I will give thanks to our Lord God and use the same method next time.

78. (6) I should not try to think of agreeable or happy things such as the glory of Heaven, the Resurrection and the like. Joyful or happy thoughts get in the way of feelings of pain, sorrow or grief for our sins. I must bear in mind that I am looking for sorrow and painful feelings, so that I ought rather to think of death and judgement.

79. (7) For the same reason, I should shut out all light, keeping shutters and doors closed whilst I am in my room, except when I have to read or take my meals.

80. (8) I should not laugh or say anything to cause laughter.

81. (9) I should control my eyes except when welcoming or taking leave of anyone I may have to speak to.

82. (10) *Penance.* This is divided into interior and exterior penance. Interior penance means sorrow for one's sins, with a firm intention of not committing them or any others.

Exterior penance, which is the outcome of this interior penance, consists in inflicting punishment on ourselves for the sins we have committed. It is of three main kinds:

83. *(a)* The first kind concerns food. When we cut out what is excessive, this is temperance, not penance.

We do penance when we cut down what is normal. The more we do this, the greater and the better is the penance, provided that the constitution is not undermined and no obvious weakness ensues.

84. *(b)* The second kind concerns sleep. Here again, it is not penance to do away with anything excessively luxurious or soft. Penance consists in cutting down what is normal in our sleeping habits, and the more we cut down the better, provided the constitution is not undermined and no obvious weakness ensues. But we should not shorten our normal time for sleeping, unless perhaps to reach the mean, if we have got into a bad habit of sleeping too much.

85. *(c)* The third form is to chastise the body by inflicting actual pain on it. This is done by wearing hairshirts or cords or iron chains, by scourging or beating ourselves and by other kinds of harsh treatment.

NOTES

86. (1) The safest and most suitable form of penance seems to be that which causes pain in the flesh but does not penetrate to the bones, that is, which causes suffering but not sickness. So the best way seems to be to scourge oneself with thin cords which hurt superficially, rather than to use some other means which might produce serious internal injury.

87. (2) The chief purpose in external penances is to produce three results:

(a) satisfaction for former sins;

(b) to overcome oneself, *i.e.* to subject the sensual nature to reason, and in general to ensure that all our lower appetites are under the control of our higher powers;

(c) to ask for and to obtain some favour or gift which one earnestly desires: for example, one may wish to have true sorrow for sins and to grieve over them; or over the pains and sorrows which Christ our Lord endured in His Passion, or to solve some doubt one is experiencing.

88. (3) Additional Practices 1 and 2 refer to the midnight and early morning exercises, but not to those at other times. No. 4 is not to be observed in church in presence of others, but only in private, at home, etc.

89. (4) When the retreatant has not yet found what he is looking for, e.g., grief, comfort, etc., it often helps if he makes some change in his penances, as regards sleep, food or other things. Thus we can modify our practice by doing penance for two or three days and then omitting it for two or three more, because it suits some to do more penance, others less. Moreover, we often leave off penance out of love of bodily comfort, judging wrongly that our constitution cannot stand it without serious illness; on the other hand, we sometimes go too far, thinking that the body can bear it. As our Lord God understands our nature infinitely better than we do, He very often enables each one, through these variations, to realize what best suits him.

90. (5) The particular examination of conscience is to be made to eliminate faults and slackness in the performance of the exercises and the additional practices. This applies also to the second and third weeks.

SECOND WEEK

THE KING

THE CALL OF THE EARTHLY KING HELPS IN THE CONTEM-
PLATION OF THE LIFE OF THE ETERNAL KING

91. THE preparatory prayer will be as usual.

First preliminary. A picture of the scene. Here it will be to see in imagination the synagogues, towns and hamlets through which Christ our Lord went preaching.

Second preliminary. To ask the grace I want. Here I ask our Lord the grace not to be deaf to His summons, but ready and enthusiastic to carry out His holy purpose.

92. *First heading.* I imagine a temporal king, chosen by our Lord God, revered and obeyed by the rulers and all the common men of Christendom.

93. *Second heading.* See how this king addresses all his followers, saying: I am determined to bring under my control the entire land of the unbeliever. Anyone, then, who wishes to join me must be satisfied to eat the food I eat, to drink what I drink, to dress as I dress; by day he will have to work alongside me, and take his turn with me at keeping a look-out by night; there will be other such things. But his share in my triumph will be proportionate to his share in my hardships.

94. *Third heading.* Think what response loyal subjects must make to a king so generous and so understanding: equally, were one to refuse the appeal of such a king, how he would incur the reprobation of all mankind and be regarded as a disgraceful coward.

95. The second part of this exercise consists in relating this illustration of the earthly king to Christ our Lord, point for point.

First heading. If we cannot ignore such a challenge, issued to his followers by an earthly king, how much more worthy of our attention is that of Christ our Lord, the Eternal King, as He confronts the whole world: to each and all He issues His summons in these words: I am determined to bring under my control the whole world and all my enemies, and so to come to the glory of my Father. To anyone, then, who chooses to join me, I offer nothing but a share in my hardships; but if he follows me in suffering he will assuredly follow me in glory.

96. *Second heading.* We realize that anyone possessed of right reason will offer himself totally for the task.

97. *Third heading.* Those who are anxious to show greater enthusiasm still and distinguish themselves in unstinted service of their eternal King and Lord of the universe, will not be content to offer themselves without reservation for the enterprise. Going against their natural weakness and their love of the world and of the flesh, they will make their dedication of themselves still more valuable and worthwhile, in these terms:

98. Eternal Lord of the Universe, in the presence of Your own infinite goodness, of Your glorious Mother and all the saints of Heaven's court, by Your grace and help, I make this my offering: I intend and desire, and it is my deliberate resolve, granted it be for the more perfect service and greater praise of Your Majesty, to imitate You in putting up with all injustice, all abuse, all poverty in reality no less than in the spirit, should Your Most Sacred Majesty be willing to choose and admit me to this state of life.

99. (*Note 1*. This exercise is to be made twice in the day, namely, on getting up in the morning and an hour either before the midday meal or before supper.)

100. (*Note 2*. For the second week and after, it will be very useful to read at times from the *Imitation of Christ* or the Gospels and from Saints' lives.)

FIRST DAY

FIRST CONTEMPLATION

THE INCARNATION

101. *After the preparatory prayer and three preliminaries there are three headings and a colloquy.*

The usual preparatory prayer.

102. *First preliminary.* The story. Here it is how the Three Divine Persons look down on the entire round of the earth's surface, filled with human beings. Seeing them all going to Hell, they decree in their eternity that the Second Person shall become man to save mankind. When the fullness of time comes they send the angel Gabriel to our Lady [§ 262].

103. *Second preliminary.* The picture. Here it means seeing the great extent of the round earth, containing so many different races: and then I must look at the room in our Lady's house at Nazareth in Galilee.

104. *Third preliminary.* Asking for what I want. Here I must ask for deep-felt knowledge of our Lord, made man for me, that I may the better love and follow Him.

105. *Note.* The preparatory prayer is the same and remains unchanged, as was said at the beginning; the three preliminaries are also the same during this and the following weeks, with such modifications as the subject-matter calls for.

106. *First heading.* See the different persons:
(1) Those on earth, with all their variety of dress

and behaviour, white and black, at peace or war, crying or laughing, well or ill, being born or dying, etc.

(2) The Three Divine Persons, seated on the royal throne proper to their Divine Majesty. They are watching the great round of the earth's surface, with all its people in a great blindness, going to Hell when they die.

(3) Our Lady, greeted by the angel.

Reflecting on what I see, I will derive some benefit.

107. *Second heading.* Listen to what is being said by the people on the earth's surface, talking to each other, swearing and blaspheming, etc.

Next, listen to what the Divine Persons are saying: "Let us bring about the redemption of mankind..."

Finally, the words of the angel and our Lady.

Reflecting on what I hear, I will derive some benefit.

108. *Third heading.* See what the people on earth are doing—wounding and killing and going to Hell...

Similarly, what the Divine Persons are doing, that is, bringing about the Incarnation and all that it means.

So, too, what the angel and our Lady are doing, namely, the one fulfilling his function as messenger, our Lady manifesting her complete submission and giving thanks to the Divine Majesty.

My reflecting on all this will benefit me in every detail.

109. *Colloquy.* Close with a colloquy, thinking out what to say to the Three Divine Persons or to the Eternal Word made flesh, or to His Mother and our Lady. According as each one is inspired, he should beg to be enabled to follow and imitate closely our Lord thus newly incarnate.

Say the *Our Father.*

SECOND CONTEMPLATION

THE NATIVITY

110. THE usual preparatory prayer.

111. *First preliminary.* The story. Our Lady, in the ninth month of her pregnancy, sets out for Nazareth riding, as we may devoutly picture her, on a donkey, accompanied by Joseph and a servant-girl, leading an ox. They are going to Bethlehem to pay the tax which Ceasar had levied on all this territory [§ 264].

112. *Second preliminary.* The picture. Represent to yourself in imagination the road from Bethlehem, in its length and breadth. Is it level or through valleys or over hillsides?

In the same way, study the place of the Nativity. Is the cave spacious or cramped, low or high? How is it furnished?

113. *Third preliminary.* The same as in the preceding contemplation and in the same form.

114. *First heading.* Look at the persons, our Lady, St Joseph, the servant-girl and, after He is born, the Infant Jesus. I must see myself as an impoverished attendant, not fit to be there, but watching and studying them, looking after all their wants as if I were actually present, in a spirit of complete and respectful subservience.

Then I should think of myself to derive some benefit.

115. *Second heading.* See, observe and study what they are saying. Then think of myself, to derive some benefit.

116. *Third heading.* See and reflect on what they are

doing. Here it is the journey they have to make, the hardships they have to put up with, before our Lord is born in utter destitution. After all His labours, after suffering from hunger and thirst, heat and cold, being treated with injustice and insulted, He is to die on the Cross—and all for me. Thinking of all this, I will derive some benefit for my soul.

117. End with a colloquy as in the preceding contemplation, and with an *Our Father*.

THIRD CONTEMPLATION

A REPETITION OF THE FIRST AND SECOND EXERCISES

118. THIS repetition begins with the preparatory prayer and the three preliminaries. Attention should always be paid to the more significant passages, where the retreatant has learnt something or has experienced comfort or distress. So, too, he should end with a colloquy and an *Our Father*.

119. In this and the succeeding repetitions, the same procedure is to be followed as in those of the previous week, changing the content but preserving the form.

FOURTH CONTEMPLATION

120. A repetition of the first and second exercises, made as above.

FIFTH CONTEMPLATION

AN APPLICATION OF THE FIVE SENSES TO THE FIRST AND SECOND CONTEMPLATIONS

121. AFTER the preparatory prayer and the three preliminaries, profit will be gained from the following imaginative use of the five senses in connection with the first and second contemplations.

122. *First heading. Look* in imagination at the persons, meditating and studying in detail the situation in which they find themselves, drawing some profit from the sight.

123. *Second heading. Listen* to what they are saying or might say. Turning to myself, I will derive some benefit.

124. *Third heading. Smell* the indescribable fragrance and *taste* the boundless sweetness of the divinity. Apply the same senses to the virtues and other qualities of soul, in different degrees.

Turning finally to myself, I will derive some profit.

125. *Fourth heading. Touch* by kissing and clinging to the places where these persons walk or sit, always trying to profit thereby.

126. At the end, as in the first and second contemplations, there should be a colloquy and an *Our Father*.

NOTES

127. (1) Throughout this week and those that follow, I must read only the event which forms the subject-matter of the contemplation immediately due. That is to say, for the present I must not read any event which I am not to study that day or at that time, since thoughts suited to one incident may get in the way of thoughts suited to another.

128. (2) The first exercise (on the Incarnation) will be made at midnight, the second at sunrise, the third at the time of Mass, the fourth at the time of Vespers, and the fifth before supper-time. An hour is to be spent on each exercise. This arrangement is to be kept to on all the following days.

129. (3) If the retreatant is elderly or weak or if, though normally strong, the first week has left him rather weakened, it is better for him, during this second week, at least sometimes, not to get up at midnight. In that case he should make one contemplation in the early morning, the next at Mass-time, and the third before the midday meal; there should be another repetition at the time of Vespers and an application of the senses before supper.

130. (4) In the second week, out of the ten Additional Practices listed during the first week, the second, sixth, seventh and part of the tenth are to be modified.

The second: As soon as I wake up, I should set before my mind the contemplation I have to make, with the desire of a greater knowledge of the Eternal Word, that I may serve and imitate Him better.

The sixth: Frequently to recall the events of the life of Christ our Lord from the time of the Incarnation to the place or event that I am due to study.

The seventh: The retreatant should keep his room light or dark, go out in fine weather or the reverse, according as he feels he will get benefit and help in finding what he wants.

The tenth: In this matter the retreatant should conduct himself as is called for by the events he is contemplating; some demand penance, some not.

In fact, all the ten Additional Practices should be observed with meticulous care.

131. (5) Apart from the midnight and early morning exercises, a practice equivalent to the second should be observed, thus: as soon as I remember that it is time for the exercise I have to perform, before going to it I should remind myself where I am going and into whose presence, briefly recalling the subject-matter: then, observing the third Practice, I will start the exercise.

SECOND DAY

132. FIRST and second contemplations on the Presentation in the Temple [§ 268] and the Flight into Exile in Egypt [§ 269], followed by two repetitions and an application of the five senses as yesterday.

133. *Note.* It sometimes helps the retreatant, even when he is strong and well disposed, to make a change for this second day until the fourth (inclusive), the better to find what he wants. He may take one contemplation at sunrise and one at Mass-time, with a repetition of them at the time for Vespers and the application of the senses before supper.

THIRD DAY

134. THE obedience of the Child Jesus to His parents [§ 271] and the Finding in the Temple [§ 272], followed by two repetitions and the application of the senses.

INTRODUCTION
TO AN EXAMINATION OF DIFFERENT STATES OF LIFE

135. THE example set us by Christ our Lord concerning the first state of life—the observance of the Commandments—has now been studied in the con-

templation on His obedience to His parents. So, too,
with regard to the second state—that of evangelical
perfection—He has given us an example in staying
behind in the Temple, leaving His foster-father and
His Mother, to devote Himself entirely to the business
of his Eternal Father. We now go on studying His
life, at the same time examining and enquiring in
what state of life His Divine Majesty wishes to make
use of us too.

By way of introduction to this enquiry, the next
exercise shows us the plan of Christ our Lord, and by
contrast that of the enemy of mankind. We shall thus
see how we ought to be preparing ourselves to achieve
perfection in whatever state of life our Lord God shall
grant us to choose.

FOURTH DAY

MEDITATION ON TWO STANDARDS

136. *One is that of Christ our Lord, our Commander-in-Chief; the other that of Lucifer, our human nature's deadly enemy.*
The usual preparatory prayer.

137. *First preliminary.* The story. Christ invites all men, desiring them to rally to His standard, whilst Lucifer, on the other side, invites them to join his.

138. *Second preliminary.* The picture. A great plain, comprising the entire Jerusalem district, where is the supreme Commander-in-Chief of the forces of good, Christ our Lord: another plain near Babylon, where Lucifer is, at the head of the enemy.

139. *Third preliminary.* Prayer for my special need.

This time it is to ask for an understanding of the tricks of the wicked leader, and for help to guard against them: also for an understanding of the life of truth exemplified by our true Commander-in-Chief; also for grace to imitate Him.

140. *First heading*. Imagine that leader of all the enemy, in that great plain of Babylon, sitting on a sort of throne of smoking flame, a horrible and terrifying sight.

141. *Second heading*. Watch him calling together countless devils, to despatch them into different cities till the whole world is covered, forgetting no province or locality, no class or single individual.

142. *Third heading*. Study the harangue he makes to them, telling them to have their traps and fetters in position, tempting men first with eagerness for money (his usual procedure) as the easiest means to acquiring some worthless position in the world, and eventually to overweening pride. Notice the three steps, money, position, pride: from these three steps he leads men on to all other vices.

143. By contrast we must make a parallel application of the imagination to our true Commander-in-Chief, Christ our Lord.

144. *First heading*. Study the attitude of Christ our Lord in that great plain in the Jerusalem country, his unostentatious manner, his attractive and delightful appearance.

145. *Second heading*. Watch the Lord of the entire world choosing so many as apostles, disciples and so on, and sending them out through the whole world, sowing the seed of His sacred teaching in the hearts of men of every rank and condition.

146. *Third heading.* Study the sermon which Christ our Lord preaches to all who serve Him and are His friends, as He sends them out on this expedition. He exhorts them to make it their aim to help everybody, leading them first to perfect poverty in the spirit, and even to poverty in reality, if this be His Divine Majesty's pleasure and He should, of His graciousness, so choose them; then to want to be laughed at and looked down on. From these two comes humility. Notice the three steps: poverty, as against money: being laughed at and looked down on as against being looked up to by men of the world: humility, as against pride. From these three steps men can be led on to all the virtues.

147. *Colloquy.* One colloquy with our Lady, asking her to get me from her Son and Lord the favour of being admitted under His standard, at first in perfect poverty in the spirit, and then in real poverty, should this be His Divine Majesty's pleasure and He should, of His graciousness, so choose me; next, in putting up with being laughed at and treated unjustly, so that I may be more like Him—so long as I can have these to bear without sin on anybody's part and offence to the Divine Majesty. I will then say a *Hail Mary*.

Second colloquy. I will ask the Son too to get me the same favour from the Father. I will then say the *Anima Christi*.

Third colloquy. I will ask the Father to give me the same favour and will say the *Our Father*.

148. *Note.* This exercise is to be made at midnight and again in the early morning. Two repetitions of it should be made at the times for Mass and Vespers, always finishing with the three colloquies with our Lady, the Son and the Father.

The following exercise on the Groups of Men is to be made before supper the same day.

THREE GROUPS OF MEN

149. ON the same fourth day is to be made a meditation on three groups of men so that I may join the best.

The usual preparatory prayer.

150. *First preliminary.* The story. This is about three groups of men, each of which has come into the possession of 10,000 ducats. Though they have acquired this money not purely and simply for the love of God, yet they are all anxious to save their souls and to be able to look at God our Lord with an easy conscience. For this they will have to get rid of the serious difficulty that arises from their attachment to their gain.

151. *Second preliminary.* The picture. Here it is to see myself standing before our Lord God and all His saints, so that I may desire and discover what is His Divine Majesty's greater pleasure.

152. *Third preliminary.* Prayer for my special need. Here it is to ask for grace to choose what is more for the glory of His Divine Majesty and my own salvation.

153. *First group.* The first group would like to be rid of their attachment to their gains, so that they may be at peace with our Lord God, and be assured of salvation. They take no steps until the moment of death.

154. *Second group.* This group also would like to rid themselves of their attachment, but in such a way that they are left with what they have got. In other words, they expect God to go the way they want and are not determined to give up what they have and make their way to God, though this would be the better state of affairs for them.

155. *Third group.* The third group are anxious to get rid of the attachment but in such a way that they do not have any preference for keeping or giving up their gains. Their whole aim is to choose or not to choose to keep them, according as our Lord God leads them to choose, as seems more in keeping with the service and praise of His Divine Majesty. Meanwhile they are of a mind to assume that they have already, in intention, given up the whole sum. They do all they can to make sure that they will not desire that or anything else at all, except when they are moved by the pure service of our Lord God. In other words, it is the simple desire of being more able to serve our Lord God which leads them to give up or to keep the thing in question.

156. *Colloquies.* The same three colloquies as in the previous contemplation on Two Standards.

157. *Note.* When we feel some attachment opposed to poverty in reality, or some distaste for it, so that our attitude is not one of strict impartiality about being poor or rich, it is a great help towards stamping out this undue attachment to beg in our colloquies (even against our natural inclination) that Christ our Lord will choose us for real poverty. This is our desire and this is what we beg and entreat for, provided it be our way of serving and praising His Divine Goodness.

FIFTH DAY

158. CONTEMPLATION on the departure of Christ our Lord from Nazareth, to go to the river Jordan to be baptized [§ 273].

NOTES

159. (1) This contemplation is to be made once at midnight and once in the early morning, with repetitions at the time of Mass and Vespers, applying the senses to it before supper. Each of these exercises should begin with the preparatory prayer and the three preliminaries, according to the instructions given fully in the contemplations on the Incarnation and the Nativity. They should end with the three colloquies of the Three Groups meditation, possibly making use of the Note appended to that exercise.

160. (2) The particular examination after the midday meal and after supper should be about my faults of slackness in the performance of the exercises and the additional practices of this day; and so of the following days.

SIXTH DAY

161. CONTEMPLATION on our Lord's leaving the Jordan for the desert and what happened there, keeping the same order as on the fifth day [§ 274].

SEVENTH DAY

ST Andrew and the others follow our Lord [§ 275].

EIGHTH DAY

THE Sermon on the Mount, on the eight beatitudes [§ 278].

NINTH DAY

OUR Lord appears to His disciples on the waves [§ 280].

TENTH DAY

OUR Lord preaches in the Temple [§ 288].

ELEVENTH DAY

THE raising of Lazarus from the dead [§ 285].

TWELFTH DAY

PALM Sunday [§ 287].

NOTES

162. (1) THIS week may be lengthened or shortened by anyone, according as he wishes to give the time to the contemplations or according to his progress. To lengthen it, if he wishes, he can take the events of our Lady's Visit to St Elizabeth, the Shepherds, the Circumcision of the Child Jesus, the Three Kings, and others too. To shorten it, he may omit some of those laid down. They have been put here by way of introduction, to give a method for better and fuller study later on.

163. (2) The matter for the Decision will begin with the Nazareth to Jordan contemplation, that is, on the fifth day [*see below*].

164. (3) Before beginning the Decision, in order to have the right attitude of mind, in accordance with the genuine teaching of Christ our Lord, it is very useful to pay close attention to the following three ways of subjection, reflecting on them intermittently all day long, and making the three colloquies, as is explained below.

THREE WAYS OF SUBJECTION

165. THE first way of subjection is necessary for salvation. It consists in my subjecting and abasing myself as far as I can, so that I always obey the law of God our Lord, at least to this extent: even if men were to offer to make me Lord of the entire creation, even were my life threatened, I should yet not think of breaking any commandment, divine or human, which bound me under pain of mortal sin.

166. The second way of subjection is more perfect than the first. It means that I so submit myself that I neither seek nor desire to be rich rather than poor, I do not try to be well thought of rather than disregarded, I do not want to live many years rather than few, where the service of our Lord God and my own salvation are equally promoted: it means that I would not contemplate committing a venial sin for all creation or to escape a threat to my life.

167. The third way of subjection is the most perfect. Supposing that I have attained to the first two ways, and granted an equal measure of praise and glory to God, I desire to be poor along with Christ in poverty rather than rich, to be insulted along with Christ so grossly insulted, rather than to be thought well of:

I would rather be thought a helpless fool for the sake of Christ who was so treated, rather than to be thought wise and clever in the world's eyes.

168. *Note.* For anyone who really wants to achieve this third form of subjection, it will be very helpful to hold the three colloquies described in the Groups meditation, begging our Lord to will to choose him for this higher and more perfect subjection, if the service and praise of His Divine Majesty be equal, if not greater.

THE MAKING OF A DECISION

PREFACE

169. To ensure a sound decision about anything, my intention must be as single-minded as I can make it. The one thing I must look at is what I was created for, which is the praising of our Lord God and the saving of my soul. It follows that whatever choice I make should be made with the idea of helping myself to achieve this ultimate purpose. The end is not to be forced to suit the means, but *vice versa*.

For instance, many first decide to get married, though this is only a means, and then to serve our Lord God in that state; yet it is the service of God which is the end. Again, others want to get benefices first, and after that to serve God, but in them. People like this do not go straight to God, but want God to come straight to their ill-directed ambitions, turning the end into the means and the means into an end. The thing they ought to adopt first they adopt as an afterthought, for we ought to make the desire to serve God our first objective, since this is our end; the acceptance of a benefice or marrying a wife (if that is better for me) must take second place, since these are means to that end. Hence, nothing should induce me either to adopt or to reject such means except the simple thought of serving and praising our Lord God, and saving my immortal soul.

CONTENT OF THE DECISION

This consideration is directed towards discovering the sort of things which form the subject-matter of the decision. It contains four headings and a note.

170. *First heading.* Anything we propose to make a decision about must be good, or at least not bad in itself; it should also be of positive advantage to our Holy Mother the Apostolic Church, or at least not bad and contrary to her interests.

171. *Second heading.* Some things have to be decided on once for all, such as ordination to the priesthood, marriage and the like. In other things our decision is open to change, for instance, accepting or surrendering a benefice or material possessions.

172. *Third heading.* In the case of a definitive decision which has been already made, by getting married, being ordained and so on, there is not room for further decision, since the first one cannot be unmade. Only one thing can be looked into. If the decision was not made with due objectivity and without irregular influences coming into play, one should be sorry about this, and try to live a good life in the chosen state. That sort of choice, influenced as it was by irregular and devious considerations, would not seem to be a call from God, as many erroneously think when they describe as a divine vocation a decision arrived at for devious and irregular reasons. A divine vocation is always unadulterated and crystal-clear, without any depraved element or other irregular motive.

173. *Fourth heading.* When a man has come to a decision from right and proper motives, without giving way to depraved and worldly considerations, then, even though the decision could be changed, there seems no reason for remaking it. He should make himself as perfect as possible in the state he has chosen.

174. *Note.* If a decision that can be changed was not arrived at in all sincerity and from the right motives, then it will be useful to make it in the proper way, if, that is, one really desires to produce effective results, to the great delight of our Lord God.

THREE OCCASIONS ON ANY OF WHICH A SOUND AND CORRECT DECISION MAY BE MADE

175. *First occasion.* When our Lord God is so obviously working on and drawing the will that, without hesitation or the very possibility of hesitating, the soul in such a state of devotion follows the lead given. This is the way St Paul and St Matthew behaved in following Christ our Lord.

176. *Second occasion.* When the mind is quite clear, deriving its knowledge from previous experience of comfort or distress and being versed in the art of discriminating between different spiritual influences.

177. *Third occasion.* When, in an undisturbed state of soul, one considers first what man was born for, which is the praising of our Lord God and saving his soul. Wanting this, he selects as the means to it a state of life within the Church, whatever will help him to serve his Lord and save his soul.

The soul is in an undisturbed state when it is not troubled by different spiritual influences but can make use of its natural faculties freely and in peace.

178. If a decision has not been arrived at on the first or second of the above occasions, the following two ways of making it are given for the third occasion.

FIRST WAY OF MAKING A SOUND AND RIGHT DECISION

It has six headings

First heading. Call to mind the subject to be decided on, e.g., the acceptance or refusal of some position or benefice, or something else pertaining to a decision that is capable of being altered.

179. *Second heading.* I must keep steadily before me what I was made for, namely, the praise of our Lord God and my soul's salvation. Moreover, I must maintain an attitude of impartiality, unaffected by any irregular motive, so that I am not inclined or disposed to accept rather than to give up the thing in question, or to give it up rather than to accept it. I should be like a pair of scales perfectly poised, inclined neither this way nor that. I must be entirely ready to pursue what I see to be more for God's glory and praise and for my soul's salvation.

180. *Third heading.* I must ask our Lord God that of His good pleasure He may influence my will and show me what action of mine in this matter will be more to His honour and renown. I should use my intelligence with strict honesty, and come to my decision in conformity with the holiness and good pleasure of His will.

181. *Fourth heading.* I should then carefully calculate the advantages or benefits that will accrue to me from holding the position or living in question, simply for our Lord God's praise and my soul's wellbeing; on the other hand I should calculate in the same way the dangers and disadvantages of holding it. I will do the same with the alternative, that is to say, looking at the advantages and benefits involved in not holding it, and, on the other hand, the dangers and disadvantages.

182. *Fifth heading.* After thus carefully investigating every aspect of the proposal, I will see in what direction reason points. Thus I must come to a conclusion about the proposal in the light of the greater rational factors and not on account of any natural inclination.

183. *Sixth heading.* When I have come to this decision or conclusion, I must turn to earnest prayer before our Lord God, offering this decision to be ratified by His Divine Majesty's acceptance of it, supposing that His service and praise are thereby promoted.

SECOND WAY OF MAKING A SOUND AND RIGHT DECISION

It contains four rules and a note

184. *Rule 1.* The love that is the motive inspiring this decision must be that higher love, deriving from the love of God. Hence, in making my decision, I must keep clearly in view the idea that any attraction

I may have for the thing in question, be it strong or weak, is simply for the sake of my Creator and Lord.

185. *Rule 2*. Let me think of a man unknown to me, whom I have never seen. Now, if I want him to be perfect in every way, let me think what decision I should tell him to make, to promote God's greater glory and his own spiritual perfection. Let me then take my own advice and observe the rule I am laying down for someone else.

186. *Rule 3*. Suppose I am at the point of death. What course of action would I then wish to have followed in coming to this particular decision? Let this be my rule for settling the whole business.

187. *Rule 4*. Let me ask myself how I would like to stand on the Day of Judgement. What decision would I then like to have made about this business? Knowing what rule I would then like to have kept, I will now observe it, so that then I may be filled with joy and satisfaction.

188. *Note*. I will make my decision in accordance with the foregoing rules to secure my salvation and my peace in eternity. I will then offer it to our Lord God in the way described under the sixth heading of the first way.

REFORMATION OF LIFE IN A GIVEN STATE

189. Let us realize that those who already hold some position in the Church or are married—whether they are well-to-do or not—have no decision to make about their state of life: in matters where some change might be made, they may be reluctant to make a decision. In these cases, instead of a formal decision, they may be helped by being given a plan or method for making some improvement in their individual lives in their particular situation. This can be done by considering their existence and their position in life in the light of the glory and praise of our Lord God and of their soul's salvation.

To fulfil this purpose, during that part of the retreat which deals with the ways of making a decision, each one must give considerable thought and attention to these points: how big a house and how large a domestic staff ought he to keep up? How should he manage it? What sort of example, in word and action, is he to give? What proportion of his wealth should he spend on his house and family and staff? How much on the poor and other works of charity?

In everything he does, the one thing he aims at, the one purpose he has in mind is the greater praise and glory of our Lord God. Everyone must bear in mind that progress in every department of the inner life will be proportionate to the degree in which he gives up self-love, self-seeking and self-interest.

THIRD WEEK

FIRST CONTEMPLATION

(at midnight)

190. *Christ our Lord leaves Bethany for Jerusalem: the events of the Last Supper* [§ 289]. *(It contains a preparatory prayer, three preliminaries, six headings and a colloquy.)*

The usual preparatory prayer.

191. *First preliminary*. The story. Christ our Lord in Bethany sends two disciples to Jerusalem to make the preparations for the Supper. He assists at it with the rest of His disciples. After eating the Paschal Lamb and finishing the Supper, He washes their feet. He gives them His most sacred Body and precious Blood and then speaks to them at length. Judas has already gone out to sell his Lord.

192. *Second preliminary*. The picture. See the road from Bethany to Jerusalem. Notice whether it is broad or narrow, level, and so on. So too the Supper-room. Is it a big one or a small one? Is it of one style rather than another?

193. *Third preliminary*. Asking for what I want. Here it is grief, compassion and a sense of guilt, because our Lord is on His way to suffer for my sins.

194. *First heading*. *See* the different figures at the Supper. Make comparisons with myself, and try to profit thereby.

Second heading. *Listen* to what they are saying; again profit thereby.

Third heading. Watch what they are doing and thus benefit.

195. *Fourth heading.* Reflect on what Christ is suffering in His human nature, or is prepared to suffer (according to the passage under consideration). Make a great effort at the beginning to compel myself to feel grief and sadness and even to shed tears. In the same way I must try hard in all that follows.

196. *Fifth heading.* Reflect how the Godhead remains concealed. It could wipe out its enemies, but does not, leaving the sacred Humanity to such cruel sufferings.

197. *Sixth heading.* Reflect that all this suffering is on account of my sins. What ought I to do and to suffer for Him?

198. End with a Colloquy to Christ our Lord, followed by the *Our Father*.

199. *Note.* It was stated above and to some extent made clear that in the colloquy I should combine reasoning with petition as the subject-matter may require, according as I experience temptation or comfort, according as I am aiming at this virtue or that. I may wish to develop this or that attitude of mind, to feel sad or joyful over what I am studying. Finally I will pray for what I chiefly want in some particular matter.

Thus I may hold just one colloquy with our Lord; but, if the subject-matter or my own sentiments incline me that way, I may make three, one with the Mother, one with the Son and one with the Father, using the scheme suggested in the second week, in the meditation on the Groups of Men, with the appended Note.

SECOND CONTEMPLATION

(at daybreak)

200. *From the Last Supper to the events in the Garden.*
The usual preparatory prayer.

201. *First preliminary.* The story. Christ our Lord,
with His eleven disciples, goes down from Mount
Sion, where the Supper has been held, to the Valley of
Josaphat. Leaving eight of them in one part of the
Valley, and three more in one part of the Garden, He
betakes Himself to prayer, His sweat turning to drops
of blood. After His enemies have fallen to the ground
at the sound of His voice, and He has been kissed
by Judas, He replaces Malchus' ear, which Peter cut
off. He is arrested like a criminal and dragged down
one face of the valley and up the other, until they come
to Annas' house.

202. *Second preliminary.* The picture. Think about
the road from Mount Sion to the Valley of Josaphat,
and then the Garden. Is it wide or long? What appearance does it have?

203. *Third preliminary.* Asking for what I want.
This is the gift proper to the Passion—sorrow in
company with Christ in His sorrow, being crushed
with the pain that crushed Christ, tears and a deep-
felt sense of suffering, because Christ suffered so
much for me.

NOTES

204. (1) This second contemplation follows the
scheme of the first (on the Supper). After the preparatory prayer and three preliminaries, the same headings
and the colloquy are employed.

Two repetitions of these two contemplations are to be made, at the time of Mass and of Vespers: before supper there is to be an application of the senses to the two foregoing contemplations, preceded always by the preparatory prayer and the three preliminaries appropriate to the subject-matter. The general scheme is that proposed and explained in the second week.

205. (2) The age, physical condition and temperament of the retreatant must determine whether all five exercises or fewer are to be made every day.

206. (3) In this third week there are certain changes in the second and sixth Additional Practices. The second: as soon as I wake up, I will recall where I am going and why, making a brief synopsis of the contemplation I have to perform. In accordance with the nature of the events, I will do my best, whilst washing and dressing, to be sad and full of grief because of the great grief and suffering of Christ our Lord.

The sixth: I will try not to evoke joyful thoughts, however good and holy, such as thoughts about the Resurrection and the glory of Heaven. I will try rather to induce in myself feelings of sorrow and pain and suffering, constantly recalling the hardships, the exhaustion and the pain which Christ our Lord endured from the moment of His birth until the particular event of the Passion which occupies my mind at present.

207. (4) The subject of the particular examination will be the exercises and Additional Practices, as in the previous week.

SECOND DAY

208. AT midnight, the contemplation will be on the events after leaving the Garden until the end of what happened in the house of Annas [§ 291].

At daybreak, from the house of Annas to the end of the events in the house of Caiphas [§ 292].

Two repetitions and the application of the senses are to be made, as stated above.

THIRD DAY

AT midnight, from the house of Caiphas to Pilate [§ 293].

At daybreak, from Pilate to Herod [§ 294].

The repetitions and the application of the senses, as described above.

FOURTH DAY

AT midnight, from Herod to Pilate [§ 295]. This contemplation should be made on the first half of the events in Pilate's residence; the rest of what happened in the same residence form the subject-matter of the exercise at daybreak. Then, as above, the repetitions and application of the senses.

FIFTH DAY

AT midnight, from Pilate's residence to the nailing to the Cross [§ 296].

At daybreak, from His being raised on the Cross until His death [§ 297].

Repetitions and application of the senses as stated.

SIXTH DAY

At midnight, from the taking down from the Cross to the preliminaries for burial [§ 298].

At daybreak, from the entombment to the house where our Lady went after her Son was buried.

SEVENTH DAY

At midnight and again at daybreak, a contemplation of the whole Passion at once.

In place of the repetitions and the application of the senses, the retreatant should reflect as often as possible throughout the day on the Sacred Body of Christ our Lord, remaining by itself separated from His soul, and on the place and manner of its burial. Similarly he should dwell on our Lady's loneliness and on her grief and exhaustion: and finally on that of the disciples.

209. *Note.* Anyone who wishes to lengthen the time spent on the Passion should take fewer events for each contemplation; for example, in the first contemplation, just the Supper; for the second, the washing of the feet; for the third, the institution of the Holy Eucharist; for the fourth, Christ's discourse; and so on for the events of the other contemplations.

In the same way, when he has finished the Passion, he can take half the story for one whole day, the second half for the next day, and the whole Passion for the third day.

On the other hand, anyone who prefers to shorten the time spent on the Passion should take the Supper at midnight, the events in the Garden at daybreak, and the events in the house of Annas at Mass-time;

at the time of Vespers, he should take the events in the house of Caiphas, and for the hour before supper what happened in Pilate's presence. By omitting the repetitions and the application of the senses in this way, he makes five separate exercises a day, each exercise including a separate event in our Lord's Passion. When he has got to the end of the whole Passion-story he could on the following day take the entire Passion together as the subject of one exercise, or divided up into several, as he thinks will be most likely to benefit him.

RULES FOR ACHIEVING SELF-CONTROL IN THE FUTURE WITH REGARD TO EATING

210. (1) THERE is not much point in cutting down on bread, which is not a food about which the appetite is usually so irregular or temptation so strong as it is about other foods.

211. (2) There is more point in cutting down on drink than on bread. So one should look carefully to see what is beneficial and to be taken, and what is bad for one and to be given up.

212. (3) Food, other than bread, calls for greater and more perfect abstinence. For it is here that the appetite inclines to excess more easily and temptation is liable to be more violent. To avoid disorder, then, in food there are two ways of practising abstinence: one, by making a practice of eating plainer foods; two, delicacies, if eaten at all, should be taken in small amounts.

213. (4) So long as he is careful to keep well, the

more a man cuts down his normal consumption, the sooner will he arrive at the proper amount of food and drink, for two reasons: *(a)* by making use of these helps and predisposing himself in this way, he will often feel to a greater extent those interior signs, comforting assurances and divine inspirations which will let him know what is the right amount for him; *(b)* if he sees that a certain degree of abstinence means that he has neither the bodily strength nor the inclination for his spiritual exercises, he will easily come to estimate what is the right amount to keep up his physical strength.

214. (5) When eating, he should pretend that he is watching Christ our Lord taking a meal with His disciples; he should study His manner of eating and drinking, looking and talking, and then try to copy Him. In this way his attention will be more taken up with thinking about our Lord and less with satisfying his bodily needs. So he will achieve greater propriety and discipline in his general conduct and deportment.

215. (6) On other occasions whilst he is eating, he can make use of other considerations, perhaps about the lives of the saints, or some devout study or some spiritual task he has to carry out. By fixing his mind on this sort of thing, he will experience less pleasurable gratification in feeding his body.

216. (7) Most of all, he should take care that his whole attention is not concentrated on his food; that, in eating, he is not carried away by his appetite; that he remains master of himself, both in the way he eats and in the amount he takes.

217. (8) One good way of regulating the appetite is

this: after the midday meal or after supper or at some time when he does not feel hungry, he should decide about his next dinner or supper, deciding every day the amount he needs to eat. This is not to be exceeded, however strong his appetite or the urge to do so. In fact, the better to control any irregularity in his appetite or any temptation from the enemy, he should eat less when he is tempted to eat more.

FOURTH WEEK

FIRST CONTEMPLATION

218. *Christ our Lord appears to our Lady* [§ 299]. The usual preparatory prayer.

219. *First preliminary*. The story. Christ has died on the Cross, and His body, though still united with the Divinity, has remained separated from His soul. His soul, now in a state of happiness and also united with the Divinity, has been down to the lower regions where He has set free the righteous souls. He then returns to the sepulchre and, rising from the dead, appears, body and soul, to His Blessed Mother.

220. *Second preliminary*. The picture. See how the tomb was arranged. See also the place, that is, the house where our Lady was, studying it in detail, her room, oratory and the rest.

221. *Third preliminary*. Prayer for my special need. Now it will be grace to be filled with joy and happiness at the thought of Christ's great glory and happiness.

222. *The first, second and third headings*. The usual ones, as in the Supper.

223. *Fourth heading*. Reflect how the Divinity, hidden, as it seemed, in the Passion, now, in the sacred Resurrection, reappears and shows its effects in truth and holiness.

224. *Fifth heading*. See Christ our Lord doing the work of consolation, comparing it with the way friends are accustomed to console one another.

225. *Colloquy*. End with one or more colloquies, according to circumstances, finally saying the *Our Father*.

226. (1) THE following contemplations go through all the events from the Resurrection onwards, including the Ascension, in the way described below. For the rest of the retreat, throughout the fourth week, the same outline and method is to be strictly observed as during the whole week of the Passion. So, in this first contemplation on the Resurrection, the preliminaries are determined by the subject-matter; so also for the five headings and the additional practices, as given below. Again, everything that remains is controlled by the pattern of the week of the Passion, as to repetitions, application of senses, shortening or lengthening the events, and so on.

227. (2) As a rule, during this fourth week, it is more appropriate than in previous ones to have four exercises and not five: the first, immediately after getting up in the morning; the second at Mass-time or before the midday meal, in place of the first repetition; the third, about the time for Vespers, in place of the second repetition; the fourth before supper, making an application of the senses to the matter of the three exercises of the day, picking out and delaying over the more important sections, and those in which the retreatant has felt more moved and spiritually refreshed.

228. (3) Whilst it is true that in all the contemplations a definite number of headings (e.g., three or five) is given, this does not mean that the person making the contemplation may not take more or fewer, according as it helps. So, before beginning the contemplation, it is worth while to look ahead and settle on a definite number of headings to be used.

229. (4) During this fourth week, out of the ten Additional Practices, changes are to be made in the second, sixth, seventh and tenth.

The second: As soon as I wake up, I must call to mind the contemplation to be made, aiming at a feeling of loving joy in the great joy and happiness of our Lord Christ.

The sixth: I will call to mind and think of such things as arouse happiness, lightheartedness and spiritual joy, such as heavenly glory.

The seventh: I will enjoy the light and the pleasure appropriate to the season, in the warmer months the coolness of shade, and in winter the warmth of the sun or of a fire, according as I am led to believe that this will help me to share the joy of my Creator and Redeemer.

The tenth: Instead of penance, I will aim at temperance and moderation in everything, apart from the fasting and abstinence commanded by the Church, which must always be kept where there is no legitimate impediment.

CONTEMPLATION FOR

ACHIEVING LOVE

230. *Note.* Two preliminary observations:
(1) Love should be expressed in doing rather than in protesting.

231. (2) Love consists in a reciprocal interchange, the lover handing over and sharing with the beloved his possessions, gifts and capacities, and *vice versa*. So, if one of them has learning, he gives it to the other who lacks it; so, too, with positions of honour or material possessions; and the other does the same.

The usual preparatory prayer.

232. *First preliminary.* The picture. I am standing in the presence of our Lord God, His angels and His saints, who are pleading for me.

233. *Second preliminary.* Asking for what I want. Here it will be to beg for a deep-felt appreciation of all the blessings I have been given, that out of the fullness of my gratitude I may become completely devoted to His Divine Majesty in effective love.

234. *First heading.* Recall the good things I have had from creation: my redemption, personal gifts. I will rouse myself to reckon how much our Lord God has done for me, how much that is His own He has shared with me; I will further consider the divine plan whereby this same Lord wants to give me all that it is in His power to give.

I then turn to myself and try to see what reason and justice demand that I offer, nay, give, His Divine Majesty in return—all that belongs to me, and with it all that I am in myself—in the spirit of one who makes a present out of a great love:

Take, Lord, into Your possession, my complete freedom of action, my memory, my understanding and my entire will, all that I have, all that I own: it is Your gift to me, I now return it to You. It is all Yours, to be used simply as You wish. Give me Your Love and Your grace; it is all I need.

235. *Second heading.* See God living in His creatures:
in matter, giving it existence,
in plants, giving them life,
in animals, giving them consciousness,
in men, giving them intelligence.

So He lives in me, giving me existence, life, consciousness, intelligence.

More, He makes me His temple, since I have been created wearing the image and likeness of God.

Again I will turn to myself, as indicated under the first heading, or in some other way that I prefer.

(This also applies to the following headings.)

236. *Third heading.* Think of God energizing, as though He were actually at work, in every created reality, in the sky, in matter, plants and fruits, herds and the like: it is He who creates them and keeps them in being, He who confers life or consciousness, and so on.

Then I turn to myself.

237. *Fourth heading.* Realize that all gifts and benefits come from above. My moderate ability comes from the supreme Omnipotence on high, as do my sense of justice, kindliness, charity, mercy, and so on, like sunbeams from the sun or streams from their source.

I will end, as was said above, by turning to myself.

In conclusion, a colloquy and an *Our Father*.

THREE WAYS OF PRAYING

I. ON THE COMMANDMENTS

238. THE first way of praying deals with the Ten Commandments, the seven deadly sins, the three powers of the soul and the five bodily senses. It is not meant to give a systematic method of prayer so much as to provide a systematic way of proceeding in certain exercises designed to prepare the soul to advance to a degree where its prayer becomes acceptable.

239. First of all, something like the second Additional Practice of the second week is to be performed; that is to say, before actually beginning to pray, my mind should rest for a time. Sitting down or walking about, as I find more helpful, I should reflect where I am going and what for. Every kind of prayer should start with this practice.

240. A preparatory prayer is to be made like this: I ask God our Lord to give me grace to recognize where I have sinned in the matter of the Ten Commandments, and so ask for the help of grace to do better for the future. I should ask for a complete understanding of them so that I may keep them better, thereby giving greater praise and glory to His Divine Majesty.

241. For this first way of praying it is useful to examine carefully the First Commandment, seeing how well I have kept it, where I have failed. As a rule, this examination should last for the time it takes to say the *Our Father* and *Hail Mary* three times. If in this space of time I find that I have committed any sins, I will aks for pardon and forgiveness, saying the *Our Father*. In this way I will go through all the Ten Commandments.

242. *Note 1.* When a man comes to think of any Commandment which he finds he is not in the habit of breaking, he need not spend so long on it. But, according to the extent to which he finds he does break it, he should spend more or less time in his study of it. The same is to be observed in examining the deadly sins.

243. *Note 2.* After completing this study of all the Commandments, recognizing his guilt in every case and asking for grace to help him to do better in future, he should conclude with a colloquy to God our Lord according to the condition in which he finds himself.

II. ON THE DEADLY SINS

244. CONCERNING the seven deadly sins, the Additional Practice and the preparatory prayer as above, with one change in the latter, since the subject-matter is sin, which is to be avoided, whereas the former exercise was concerned with commandments which are to be observed. Otherwise, the same regular scheme is to be followed, with the colloquy.

245. *Note.* In order to get a better appreciation of his failings in the matter of the deadly sins, a consideration of their contraries should be made. And so, in order to avoid the sins more effectively, he should make it his aim and care to get a habit of these seven contrary virtues, by means of devout practices.

III. ON THE POWERS OF THE SOUL

246. THE same regular scheme is to be observed in dealing with the powers of the soul, including the Additional Practice, preparatory prayer and colloquy.

IV. ON THE FIVE BODILY SENSES

247. THE same scheme is always to be used concerning the five bodily senses, changing the content.

248. *Note.* The man who wishes to use his senses as Christ used His, should commend himself to the Divine Majesty in the preparatory prayer, and after thinking about each one should say a *Hail Mary* or an *Our Father*; or one may wish to use them as our Lady used hers, in which case the commendation should be made to her, that she may obtain from her Son this special grace for the retreatant: after thinking about each sense, a *Hail Mary* should be said.

SECOND WAY OF PRAYING

249. *Dwelling on the meaning of each word of a particular prayer.*

250. *Additional Practice:* In this second way, the same Additional Practice as for the first.

251. The *preparatory prayer* should be one appropriate to the person addressed.

252. The second way of praying is as follows: Kneeling or sitting according to inclination and devotion, and with his eyes closed or fixed in one place and not turning this way and that, he should say: "Father" and go on dwelling on this word as long as he finds meaning, analogies and a sense of spiritual comfort arising from the ideas appropriate to this term. He should proceed in the same way concerning each word of the *Our Father* or whatever prayer he may choose for this way of praying.

253. *Three rules:* (1) In this way he should spend an hour on the entire *Our Father*; when it is finished he is to say the *Hail Mary*, the *Creed*, the *Anima Christi* and the *Salve Regina*, in the usual way, either vocally or mentally.

254. (2) If in dwelling on the *Our Father* he finds in one or two words abundant food for thought and a sense of spiritual comfort, he should not be anxious to move on, even if the end of the hour comes whilst he is still in that stage. At the end, he should finish off the *Our Father* in the usual way.

255. (3) If he has spent a whole hour on one or two words of the *Our Father*, when, on some other day, he wishes to come back to it, he should say this word or these two words in the ordinary way and begin his contemplation, in the way described in the second rule, at the word immediately following.

256. *Two notes:* (1) When the *Our Father* has been finished, whether on one day or several, the same procedure should be applied to the *Hail Mary*, and then to the other prayers, so that he is always engaged on one of them, over some period of time.

257. (2) At the end of the prayer, he should turn to the person to whom it was addressed, and briefly ask for those virtues or graces of which he feels the greatest need.

THIRD WAY OF PRAYING

258. *In rhythm.*

Additional Practice as in the first and second ways of praying.

Preparatory prayer as in the second way of praying.

This is the third way of praying: Every time I breathe in, I should pray mentally, saying one word of the *Our Father* (or whatever prayer is being recited), so that only one word is uttered between each breath and the next. In the space between one breath and the next, I dwell particularly on the meaning of the word, or on the person addressed, or on my own worthlessness, or on the great difference between the magnificence of that person and my own worthlessness. The same regular scheme can be applied to the rest of the *Our Father*. The other prayers, namely, the *Hail Mary, Anima Christi,* the *Creed,* and the *Salve Regina,* will be said in the ordinary way.

259. *Two rules:* (1) The next day or the next time one wishes to pray, he should recite the *Hail Mary* in this rhythmic way, and then the other prayers in the usual way; and so on through them all.

260. (2) Anyone who wishes to spend more time in this rhythmic way of praying can say all the prayers mentioned above, or some portion of them, keeping the same regular rhythm according to breathing, as explained above.

EVENTS OF THE LIFE
OF OUR LORD CHRIST

261. *Note*. In all the following events, the words in inverted commas are from the Gospel itself, but not those without inverted commas. In each event, as a rule, three headings will be found, in order to make the meditation or contemplation easier.

THE ANNUNCIATION TO OUR LADY
(Text in Luke 1. 26-38)

262. *First heading*. The angel, St Gabriel, greets our Lady, telling her of the conception of our Lord Christ. "Into her presence the angel came, and said, Hail, thou who art full of grace... thou shalt conceive in thy womb and bear a son."

Second heading. The angel corroborates what he says to our Lady by telling her of the conception of St John the Baptist in the words: "See, moreover, how it fares with thy cousin Elizabeth; she is old, yet she has conceived a son."

Third heading. Our Lady answers the angel: "Behold the handmaid of the Lord; let it be unto me according to thy word."

THE VISITATION OF OUR LADY TO ELIZABETH
(Luke 1. 39-56)

263. *First heading*. When our Lady visited Elizabeth, St John the Baptist, in his mother's womb, was aware of our Lady's visit: "No sooner had Elizabeth heard Mary's greeting than the child leaped in her womb;

and Elizabeth herself was filled with the Holy Ghost; so that she cried out with a loud voice, Blessed art thou among women, and blessed is the fruit of thy womb."

Second heading. Our Lady sings her canticle, in the words: "My soul magnifies the Lord".

Third heading. "Mary returned home when she had been with her about three months".

THE BIRTH OF CHRIST OUR LORD
(Luke 2. 1-14)

264. *First.* Our Lady and her husband, Joseph, go from Nazareth to Bethlehem. "Joseph came up from Galilee to Bethlehem... to give in his name there" to recognize his subjection to Caesar. "With him was his espoused wife Mary, who was then in her pregnancy."

Second. "She brought forth a son, her first-born, whom she wrapped in his swaddling clothes and laid in a manger."

Third. "Then, on a sudden, a multitude of the heavenly army appeared to them at the angel's side... saying, Glory to God in high heaven."

THE SHEPHERDS
(Luke 2. 8-20)

265. *First.* An angel reveals Christ's birth to the shepherds: "The news I bring you is good news of a great rejoicing... This day the Saviour of the world is born..."

Second. The shepherds go to Bethlehem: "They went with all haste, and found Mary and Joseph, with the Child lying in the manger."

Third. "The shepherds went home giving praise and glory to God."

THE CIRCUMCISION
(Luke 2. 21)

266. *First.* They circumcised the child Jesus.

Second. "He was called Jesus, the name which the angel had given him before he was conceived in the womb."

Third. They give the child back to His Mother, who was moved to compassion over the blood shed by her Son.

THE THREE MAGI-KINGS
(Matthew 2. 1-12)

267. *First.* The three Magi-Kings, led by the star, came to worship Jesus, saying: "We have seen his star out in the east and have come to worship him."

Second. They did worship him and offered him gifts:"They fell down to worship him:and they offered him gifts of gold, frankincense and myrrh."

Third. "They received a warning in a dream forbidding them to go back to Herod and returned to their own country by a different way."

THE PURIFICATION OF OUR LADY AND THE PRESENTATION OF THE CHILD JESUS
(Luke 2. 22-39)

268. *First.* They take the child Jesus to the Temple so that He may be presented to the Lord as a first-born son, and make an offering for Him: "a pair of turtledoves or two young pigeons".

Second. Simeon, coming into the Temple, "took him into his arms", saying: "Now, Lord, thou dost let thy servant go in peace".

Third. Anna "came near to give God thanks and spoke of the child to all that patiently waited for the deliverance of Israel".

THE FLIGHT INTO EGYPT
(Matthew 2. 13-15)

269. *First*. Herod, seeking to kill the child Jesus, killed the Innocent children. Before their death, the angel warned Joseph to take flight into Egypte: "Rise up, take with thee the child and his mother and flee to Egypt."

Second. He left for Egypt: "He rose up therefore, while it was still night, and... withdrew into Egypt".

Third. He stayed there until the death of Herod.

HOW OUR LORD CHRIST RETURNED FROM EGYPT
(Matthew 2. 19-23)

270. *First*. The angel warned Joseph to go back to Israel: "Rise up, take the child and his mother and return to the land of Israel."

Second. He rose up and came into the land of Israel.

Third. Because Archelaus, the son of Herod, was king in Judaea, he "withdrew" to Nazareth.

THE LIFE OF OUR LORD FROM TWELVE TO THIRTY
(Luke 2. 51-52)

271. *First*. He was obedient to His parents.

Second. He "advanced in wisdom with the years and in grace".

Third. He apparently worked as a carpenter, as St Mark seems to imply: "Is not this the carpenter?" *(Mark 6. 3)*.

CHRIST'S COMING TO THE TEMPLE AT THE AGE OF TWELVE
(Luke 2. 41-50)

272. *First.* Christ our Lord at the age of twelve went up from Nazareth to Jerusalem.

Second. Christ our Lord stayed in Jerusalem, without the knowledge of His parents.

Third. Three days later they found Him, sitting amongst the doctors in the Temple, arguing with them: to His parents' question, asking where He had been, He replied: "Could you not tell that I must needs be in the place that belongs to my Father?"

CHRIST'S BAPTISM
(Matthew 3. 13-17)

273. *First.* Christ our Lord, after saying goodbye to His blessed Mother, came from Nazareth to the banks of the Jordan, where John the Baptist was.

Second. St John baptized Christ our Lord. When he sought to excuse himself, thinking himself unfit to do this, Christ said: "Let it be so for the present; it is well that we should thus fulfil all due observance."

Third. The Holy Spirit came down on him, whilst the voice of the Father bore witness from Heaven: "This is my beloved Son, in whom I am well pleased."

THE TEMPTING OF CHRIST
(Matthew 4. 1-13)

274. *First.* After His baptism, He withdrew into the desert, where He fasted for forty days and nights.

Second. He was three times tempted by the enemy: "The tempter approached and said to him, If thou art the Son of God, bid these stones turn into loaves of bread... cast thyself down to earth... I will give thee all these if thou wilt fall down and worship me."

Third. "Angels came and ministered to him."

THE CALLING OF THE APOSTLES

275. *First.* Apparently St Peter and St Andrew were called three times: (1) to know Him in some degree (John 1); (2) to follow Him to some degree, though with the intention of returning to the possessing of what they had left (Luke 5); (3) to follow Christ our Lord permanently (Matt. 4; Mark 1).

Second. Philip was called by Him (John 1); Matthew too (Matt. 9: Mark 2).

Third. The other Apostles were called, though no mention of individual calls is made in the Gospel.

Moreover, there are three other points to be borne in mind:

(1) The Apostles were uncouth and humble in origin.

(2) The dignity to which they were so gently called.

(3) The gifts and graces which raised them above all the Fathers of the New or Old Dispensation.

THE FIRST MIRACLE, PERFORMED AT THE WEDDING AT CANA IN GALILEE
(*John 2. 1-11*)

276. *First.* Christ our Lord was invited to the wedding, together with His disciples.

Second. The mother tells her son of the shortage of wine, in the words "They have no wine left", saying to the servants, "Do whatever he tells you".

Third. He changed the water into wine and so

"made known the glory that was his, so that his disciples learned to believe in him".

CHRIST DRIVES THE HUCKSTERS OUT OF THE TEMPLE

(*John 2. 13-22*)

277. *First.* He drove out of the Temple all who were selling there, using a whip made of cords.

Second. He upset the tables and the money of the wealthy money-changers in the Temple.

Third. To the poor dove-sellers, he said gently: "Take these away. Do not turn my Father's house into a place of barter."

THE SERMON PREACHED BY CHRIST ON THE MOUNT

(*Matthew 5. 1-48*)

278. *First.* He speaks privately to His beloved disciples of the eight beatitudes: "Blessed are the poor in spirit... the patient... the merciful... those who mourn... those who hunger and thirst for holiness... the clean of heart... peacemakers... those who suffer persecution..."

Second. He exhorts them to use their talents well: "Your light must shine so brightly before men that they can see your good works and glorify your Father who is in heaven".

Third. He shows that, far from breaking the law, He is fulfilling it, explaining the commandments not to kill, not to commit adultery, not to swear falsely, and to love our enemies: "I tell you, Love your enemies, do good to those who hate you".

CHRIST CALMS THE STORM ON THE SEA
(Matthew 8. 23-27)

279. *First*. Whilst Christ our Lord was sleeping at sea, a great storm got up.

Second. His terrified disciples wake Him up. He finds fault with the weakness of their faith, in the words: "Why are you faint-hearted, men of little faith?"

Third. He orders the winds and waves to stop; when they do so, the sea falls calm, to the astonishment of the disciples who say: "What kind of man is this, who is obeyed even by the winds and the sea?"

CHRIST WALKS ON THE SEA
(Matthew 14. 22-33)

280. *First*. When He was on the mountain, Christ our Lord told His disciples to go off to the boat, sent the crowd away and began to pray alone.

Second. The boat was being tossed by the waves, when Christ approached, walking on the water. His disciples thought it was a ghost.

Third. When Christ said to them: "It is myself, do not be afraid", St Peter, at His bidding, walked towards Him on the water. But in his doubt he began to sink. Christ rescued him, upbraiding him for the weakness of his faith. As He came on board, the wind dropped.

THE APOSTLES ARE SENT OUT PREACHING
(Matthew 10. 1-42; 11. 1)

281. *First*. Christ, calling together His beloved disciples, gives them power to expel devils from men's bodies and to heal every disease.

Second. He instructs them in prudence and patience: "Remember, I am sending you out to be like sheep among wolves; you must be wary, then, as serpents and yet innocent as doves."

Third. He gives them their instructions for the journey: "Do not have gold or silver; give as you have received the gift, without payment". He also told them what to preach about: "Preach as you go, telling them, The kingdom of heaven is at hand."

MAGDALEN IS CONVERTED
(Luke 7. 36-50)

282. *First.* Magdalen goes into the Pharisee's house where Christ our Lord is at table. She is carrying an alabaster pot, full of ointment.

Second. Taking up her position behind our Lord, near His feet, she began to shed tears over them; drying them with her hair, she kissed them and put some of the ointment on them.

Third. When the Pharisee accused Magdalen, Christ spoke up in her defence: "If great sins have been forgiven her, she has also greatly loved." But He told the woman, "Thy faith has saved thee; go in peace."

CHRIST GIVES FOOD TO FIVE THOUSAND
(Matthew 14. 13-21)

283. *First.* As it is getting late, the disciples ask Christ to send away the crowd accompanying Him.

Second. Christ our Lord tells them to bring Him the loaves; telling the crowd to sit down, He blesses and breaks up the loaves, giving them to the disciples to distribute to the crowd.

Third. "All ate and had enough," and twelve basketfuls were left over.

CHRIST IS TRANSFIGURED
(St Matthew 17. 1-9)

284. *First.* Taking with Him as companions His dear disciples Peter, James and John, He was transfigured, His face bright as the sun, His garments snow-white.

Second. He conversed with Moses and Elias.

Third. Peter said: Let us pitch three tents here. A voice from heaven was heard saying, "This is my beloved Son...; to him, then, listen." On hearing this voice, His disciples were terrified and fell on their faces. Christ our Lord touched them, saying, "Arise, do not be afraid;... Do not tell anybody of what you have seen until the Son of Man has risen from the dead."

THE RAISING OF LAZARUS
(John 11. 1-45)

285. *First.* Martha and Mary tell our Lord that Lazarus is sick. After hearing this, He waited for two days, so that the miracle might be more striking.

Second. Before bringing their brother back to life, He asks both sisters to have faith, saying: "I am the resurrection and life; he who believes in me, though he is dead, will live on".

Third. After bursting into tears, he prays and raises Lazarus, ordering him in the words: "Come out, Lazarus, to my side".

4 SE

THE SUPPER AT BETHANY
(Matthew 26. 6-13)

286. *First.* Our Lord goes to supper in the house of the leper, Simon: Lazarus is also there.

Second. Mary pours the ointment on Christ's head.

Third. Judas grumbles, "What is the meaning of this waste?" But our Lord again defends Magdalen, in the words, "Why do you vex the woman? She did well to treat me so."

PALM SUNDAY
(Matthew 21. 1-11)

287. *First.* Our Lord sends for the ass and her foal, with the words: "Untie them and bring them to me. And if anyone speaks to you about it, tell him, The Lord has need of them, and he will let you have them without more ado."

Second. He mounted the ass, after it had been saddled with the Apostles' garments.

Third. People come out to welcome Him, spreading on the ground their garments or branches cut from trees, shouting: "Hosanna for the son of David, blessed is he who comes in the name of the Lord, Hosanna in heaven above."

PREACHING IN THE TEMPLE
(Luke 19. 47-48)

288. *First.* He was in the Temple every day, teaching.

Second. At the end of His preaching, as there was no one in Jerusalem to take Him in, He used to go back to Bethany.

THE SUPPER
(Matthew 26. 17-30; St John 13. 1-30)

289. *First*. He eats the paschal lamb with His disciples, to whom He foretells His death: "Believe me, one of you is to betray me".

Second. He washes the feet of His disciples, including Judas. He begins with St Peter who, at the thought of our Lord's dignity and his own worthlessness, expresses his reluctance to permit this, in the words: "Lord, is it for thee to wash my feet?" But St Peter did not realize that our Lord was giving an example of humility in this way, as He Himself said: "I have been setting you an example which will teach you in your turn to do what I have done for you".

Third. He institutes the most Holy Eucharistic sacrifice as the greatest sign of His love, in the words, "Take, eat...". At the end of the Supper, Judas goes out to sell Him.

FROM THE SUPPER TO THE EVENTS IN THE GARDEN
(Matthew 26. 30-46; Mark 14. 26-42)

290. *First*. At the end of Supper and after singing a hymn, our Lord sets out for the Mount of Olives, with His terrified disciples. He leaves eight of them in Gethsemani, with the words: "Sit down here, while I go in there and pray".

Second. Taking with Him Peter, James and John, He prays three times to God, in the words: "My Father, if it is possible, let this chalice pass me by; only as thy will is, not as mine is." In His agony, He prayed all the more earnestly.

Third. He fell into such dread that He said: "My

soul is ready to die with sorrow". And He sweated blood so abundantly that St Luke tells us: "His sweat fell to the ground like thick drops of blood", implying that His garments were already soaked.

FROM THE GARDEN TO THE HOUSE OF ANNAS
(Matthew 26. 47-58; Mark 14. 43-54, 66-68;
Luke 22. 47-57; John 18. 1-24)

291. *First*. Our Lord lets Himself be kissed by Judas and arrested as a brigand. He says to them: "You have come out to my arrest with swords and clubs as if I were a robber; I was close to you in the temple day after day and you never laid hands on me". When He said, "Who is it you are looking for?" His enemies fell to the ground.

Second. When St Peter wounded a servant of the High Priest, our Lord in his gentleness told him: "Put thy sword back into its sheath," meanwhile healing the servant.

Third. Abandoned by His disciples He is dragged off to the house of Annas, where St Peter, who had followed Him at a distance, first denied knowing Him. Christ was struck by a man, who said to Him: "Is this how thou makest answer to the high priest?"

FROM THE HOUSE OF ANNAS TO THAT OF CAIPHAS

292. *First*. From the house of Annas He is taken, with His hands bound, to the house of Caiphas. Here Peter twice more denies knowing Him, and, when our Lord looks at him, "He went out and wept bitterly".

Second. Jesus remained in fetters all that night.

Third. Furthermore, those who kept Him prisoner, made fun of Him, beat Him, and, blindfolding Him, hit Him and then asked: "Come prophesy; tell us who it is that smote thee." Other similar indignities they perpetrated on Him.

FROM THE HOUSE OF CAIPHAS TO THAT OF PILATE
(Matthew 27. 1-2, 11-26; Mark 15. 1-15;
Luke 23. 1-5, 13-24)

293. *First.* The whole crowd of the Jews take Him off to Pilate and, in the governor's presence, bring their accusations in the words: "We have discovered that this man is subverting the loyalty of our people and forbids the payment of tribute to Ceasar".

Second. Having twice examined Him, Pilate declares: "I find no fault in him".

Third. Barabbas the brigand was preferred to Him: "They all made a fresh outcry: Barabbas, they said, not this man".

FROM THE HOUSE OF PILATE TO THAT OF HEROD

294. *First.* Pilate sent Jesus, being a Galilean, to the tetrarch of Galilee, Herod.

Second. Herod, out of curiosity, questioned Him at length, but received no answer, despite the constant accusations brought by the Scribes and Pharisees.

Third. Herod and all his court showed their contempt for Him, and put on Him a white robe.

FROM THE HOUSE OF HEROD TO PILATE'S
(Matthew 27; Mark 15; Luke 23; John 19)

295. *First.* Herod sends Him back to Pilate. This creates a friendship between the two men who were previously at enmity.

Second. Pilate took Jesus and scourged Him; the

soldiers making a thorn-crown, placed it on His head, and putting a scarlet cloak on Him, came up to Him, saying: "Hail, king of the Jews" and striking Him.

Third. He brought Him out in front of the whole crowd: "Then, as Jesus came out, still wearing the crown of thorns and the scarlet cloak, he said to them, See, here is the man." When the priests had seen Him, they shouted out: "Crucify him, crucify him".

FROM PILATE'S HOUSE TO THE CRUCIFIXION
(*John* 19. 13-22)

296. *First*. From his judgement-seat, Pilate hands Jesus over to the Jews to be crucified, after they have denied His kingship, in the words: "We have no king but Caesar".

Second. Jesus carries the Cross on His shoulders, until He can no longer carry it, when Simon of Cyrene is forced to carry it behind Jesus.

Third. They crucify Him between two brigands, affixing the title: "Jesus of Nazareth, King of the Jews".

ON THE CROSS
(*John* 19. 23-37)

297. *First*. The seven words which He speaks when hanging on the Cross: a prayer for those who were crucifying Him; pardon for the brigand; St John commended to His Mother and His Mother to St John; "I thirst", followed by the offer of gall and vinegar; cry of abandonment; "It is achieved"; "Father, into thy hands I commend my spirit".

Second. The darkening of the sun, the splitting of

rocks, opening of tombs, rending of the Temple veil from top to bottom.

Third. Blasphemies uttered against Him, in the words: "Come now, thou who wouldst destroy the Temple of God... come down from the cross"; the dividing up of His garments; the piercing of His side with a lance, and the flow of blood and water.

FROM CROSS TO TOMB
(John 19. 38-42)

298. *First.* He is taken down from the Cross by Joseph and Nicodemus, before the eyes of his grief-stricken mother.

Second. His body is carried to the tomb, anointed and buried.

Third. Guards are posted.

OUR LORD'S RESURRECTION AND FIRST APPEARANCE

299. *First.* He appeared to His Virgin Mother: it is true that this is not explicitly mentioned in Scripture, but it is implied in the passage which says that He appeared to so many others. For Scripture presumes that we possess understanding, in the words: "Are you too still lacking in understanding?"

THE SECOND APPEARANCE
(Mark 16. 1-11)

300. *First.* Very early in the morning, Mary Magdalen and the mother of James, and Salome go to the tomb, saying: "Who is to roll away the stone for us from the door of the tomb?"

Second. They find the stone rolled away and nearby

an angel, who says: "You have come to look for Jesus
of Nazareth...; he has risen again; he is not here".

Third. He appears to Mary who stayed behind near
the tomb after the others had gone.

THE THIRD APPEARANCE
(Matthew 28. 8-10)

301. *First.* The other two called Mary leave the
tomb in fear and great rejoicing, with the intention
of telling the disciples of the Lord's Resurrection.

Second. Christ our Lord appeared to them on the
way with the words: "All hail". They came near and
fell down at His feet to worship Him.

Third. Jesus says to them: "Do not be afraid; go and
give word to my brethren to remove into Galilee; they
will see me there".

THE FOURTH APPEARANCE
(Luke 24. 9-12, 33-34)

302. *First.* On hearing from the women that Christ
had risen again, St Peter quickly went to the tomb.

Second. Going in, he saw nothing but the linen
with which the body of Christ had been covered.

Third. Whilst St Peter is pondering on all this,
Christ appeared; hence the disciples said: "The Lord
has indeed risen, and has appeared to Simon".

THE FIFTH APPEARANCE
(Luke 24. 13-34)

303. *First.* He appears to the disciples on their way
to Emmaus, whilst they are talking about Christ.

Second. He finds fault with them, making it clear

from the Scriptures that Christ had to suffer and rise again: "Too slow of wit, too dull of heart, to believe all those saying of the prophets!... Was it not to be expected that Christ should undergo these sufferings and enter so into his glory?"

Third. At their entreaty He stays there, remaining until, having given them communion, He disappears: they themselves, going back, told the disciples how they had come to know Him in communion.

THE SIXTH APPEARANCE
(John 20. 19-23)

304. *First.* The disciples were gathered in a body "for fear of the Jews", with the exception of St Thomas.

Second. Although the doors were shut, Jesus appeared to them; standing in the middle of them He said: "Peace be upon you."

Third. He gives them the Holy Spirit, with these words to them: "Receive the Holy Spirit; when you forgive men's sins they are forgiven."

THE SEVENTH APPEARANCE
(John 20. 24-29)

305. *First.* St Thomas, having been absent on the occasion of the previous appearance, refuses to believe and says: "Unless I see... I will not believe".

Second. A week later, the doors again being closed, Jesus appears to them and says to St Thomas: "Let me have thy finger; see... Cease thy doubting and believe."

Third. St Thomas believes and says: "My Lord and my God". Christ says to him: "Blessed are they who have not seen and have believed."

THE EIGHTH APPEARANCE

(*John 21. 1-17*)

306. *First.* Jesus appears to seven of His disciples whilst they are fishing, having caught nothing the whole night. They cast their net at His command and "found they had no strength to haul it in, such a shoal of fish was in it".

Second. Through this miracle, St John recognized Him and said to St Peter: "It is the Lord". Peter immediately jumps into the sea and comes to Christ.

Third. He gave them to eat a portion of broiled fish and a honeycomb. After testing St Peter's charity three times, He commends to him the sheep in the words: "Feed my sheep".

THE NINTH APPEARANCE

(*Matthew 28. 16-20*)

307. *First.* By our Lord's command the disciples go to Mount Thabor.

Second. Christ appears to them and says: "All authority on heaven and earth has been given to me".

Third. He sends them to preach throughout the whole world, with the words: "Go out, making disciples of all nations, and baptizing them in the name of the Father and of the Son and of the Holy Ghost"

THE TENTH APPEARANCE

(*1 Cor. 15. 6*)

308. "Then he was seen by more than five hundred of the brethren at once."

THE ELEVENTH APPEARANCE

(1 Cor. 15. 7)

309. "Then he was seen by James."

THE TWELFTH APPEARANCE

310. In our meditation we may piously think of His appearance to Joseph of Arimathea, as told in the lives of the saints.

THE THIRTEENTH APPEARANCE

(1 Cor. 15. 8)

311. He appeared to St Paul after the Ascension: "And last of all, I, too, saw him, like the last child that comes to birth unexpectedly". He appeared in His soul to the holy fathers in Limbo. After leading them out from there, and taking His body again, He often appeared to His disciples, holding converse with them.

THE ASCENSION OF CHRIST OUR LORD

(Acts 1. 1-12)

312. *First.* After appearing to the Apostles over a period of forty days, producing many proofs and portents and talking to them about the Kingdom of God, He told them to wait in Jerusalem for the promised Holy Spirit.

Second. Leading them out to Mount Olivet, He was lifted up before their eyes until a cloud took Him away from their sight.

Third. As they went on looking up into Heaven, angels address them: "Men of Galilee, why do you stand here looking heavenwards? He who has been taken from you into heaven, this same Jesus, will come back in the same fashion, just as you have watched him going into heaven."

RULES FOR DISTINGUISHING
BETWEEN DIFFERENT
SPIRITUAL INFLUENCES

SO THAT ONLY GOOD ONES MAY BE ADMITTED, EVIL ONES
BEING REJECTED

I

(More suitable for the first-week exercises)

314. (1) Those who go from mortal sin to mortal sin are usually influenced in this way: the enemy proposes certain illusory delights, causing them to imagine sensual pleasures and enjoyments, the more effectively to keep them under the sway of their vicious and sinful course. The good spirit deals with these same people in the opposite way, working on their consciences by reason to induce compunction and remorse.

315. (2) The contrary prevails with those who are making earnest progress in self-purification, rising from good to better in the service of God our Lord. In these cases it is typical of the evil spirit to cause regret and sadness, using fallacious arguments to disturb them and impede their progress. On the other hand, the role of the good spirit is to provide courage and strength, to console and inspire, to move to tears, all in a spirit of peace. Everything is made easy, all obstacles are removed, to enable the soul to continue in virtue.

316. (3) Spiritual comfort: this is the name I give to any interior movement experienced by the soul, causing it to glow with love for its Creator and Lord, the effect of which is that it can no longer love any earthly creature in itself, but only in the Creator of them all. The name also applies to the shedding of tears leading to love of God, either out of sorrow for sin or for the sufferings of Christ our Lord, or for other reasons directly concerned with His service and praise. Lastly, comfort is the name given to any growth in faith, hope or charity, or to any inward joy which summons or draws a man to the things of the next world, to the saving of his own soul, bringing the soul to peace and tranquillity in its Creator and Lord.

317. (4) Spiritual distress: this is the name I give to whatever is opposite to the foregoing—darkness of soul, disquiet of mind, an attraction to what is coarse and earthly, all restlessness proceeding from different temptations and disturbances, such as the temptation tending to destroy faith, hope and charity; the condition in which the soul finds itself listless, apathetic, melancholy, like one cut off from its Creator and Lord. Inasmuch as comfort and distress are opposed, the thoughts that spring from the former are contrary to those springing from the latter.

318. (5) In a period of distress we are not to alter anything, but should remain firm and unyielding in our resolutions and the purpose of mind in which we found ourselves on the day preceding such distress, or in the purpose in which we found ourselves in the preceding comfort. For in times of comfort it is the good spirit that guides us by his counsel, whereas in distress it is the evil spirit; but the latter's counsel will never bring us to a right decision.

319. (6) Though in principle we should not alter

our previous resolutions in periods of distress, it is of great value to strive in a sense opposed to the distress; for instance by more insistence on prayer, meditation, close examination, and by making an effort to practise some appropriate penance.

320. (7) When in distress, a man should reflect that God is testing him by leaving him to his own resources in his struggle against the different assaults and temptations of the enemy; he can succeed with the help of God, which is always there, even though he is not clearly aware of it. God has indeed withdrawn any great warmth of feeling, intensity of love and extraordinary grace, but He has left grace enough for the man's eternal salvation.

321. (8) In this state he should also strive to abide in patience, which is the antidote to the trials that beset him. He should also reflect that he will soon be comforted, and should put forth all his efforts against this distress, as described in the sixth rule.

322. (9) There are three chief reasons why we experience distress:

(a) Because we are listless, apathetic and careless in our spiritual exercises; it is on account of our own faults that our spiritual comfort is withdrawn.

(b) To test our worth, and to show how far we are able to advance in His service and praise without that great reward of comforts and extraordinary favours.

(c) To give us clear understanding and insight, to enable us to have a deep inner conviction that of ourselves we are powerless to produce or sustain a flood of devout feelings, intense love, tears or any other spiritual comfort, but that this is all a gratuitous gift of God our Lord. We are not, that is, to build on

another's foundations, getting above ourselves in pride and empty boasting, claiming as our own the devout feelings or other features of spiritual comfort.

323. (10) In a period of comfort a man should think about his conduct in the distress that will ensue, building up his strength afresh for that experience.

324. (11) When experiencing comfort he should be careful to keep himself humble and modest, recalling how worthless he is in time of distress, when he is without the favour of this comfort. Contrariwise, a man who is in a state of distress should reflect that he can do a great deal with the grace that is sufficient to withstand all his enemies, finding strength in his Creator and Lord.

325. (12) The enemy is like a woman, weak in face of opposition, but correspondingly strong when not opposed. In a quarrel with a man, it is natural for a woman to lose heart and run away when he faces up to her; on the other hand, if the man begins to be afraid and to give ground, her rage, vindictiveness and fury overflow and know no limit. In the same way, it is typical of the enemy to collapse and lose heart, his assaults turning tail, when a man who is training himself in spirituality faces up to the enemy's assaults, doing the precise opposite to what is suggested. On the other hand, if the retreatant begins to feel panic and to lose heart at these assaults, there is no animal on earth so savage as is the enemy of our human nature in the ever-growing malice with which he carries out his evil plan.

326. (13) He is also like a seducer in his desire to remain disguised and undetected. If that sort of schemer pays dishonourable court to the daughter of a good father or the wife of a good husband, he wants his words and suggestions not to be disclosed; he is greatly upset if the daughter or the wife tells the father or the husband about his deceitful words and his dishonourable purpose, since he easily recognizes that he will not then realize the plan he has embarked on.

So is it with the enemy of our human nature. When he introduces into a faithful soul his lying suggestions, he is very anxious that these should be accepted and kept secret. But he is far from pleased when their victim discloses them to a good confessor or someone else versed in spiritual matters, who is acquainted with the ill-disposed designs of the tempter, who then realizes that his wicked attempt must fail, once his obvious tricks are revealed.

327. (14) Or again he acts like a military commander in his attempts to overcome and seize the object he has set his heart on. An officer in command of an army takes up a position, makes a reconnaissance to discover the strength and disposition of troops in a fortified post and launches his attack at the weakest point. Similarly, the enemy of our human nature makes a tour of inspection of our virtues—theological, cardinal and moral. Where he finds us weakest and most defective in what pertains to our eternal salvation, he attacks at that point, seeking to overthrow us.

II

328. Rules for the same purpose, with a more precise way of distinguishing between different spiritual influences. These rules are more appropriate to the second week.

329. (1) The characteristic effect produced by God and His angels in their spiritual operations is a genuine lightness of heart and spiritual joy, eliminating all the disturbing sadness engendered by the enemy, whilst his characteristic activity is to resist such lightness of heart and spiritual comfort, alleging specious reasons, subtle suggestions and sophistries without end.

330. (2) Spiritual comfort with no previous occasion giving rise to it comes from our Lord God alone. It is the Creator's prerogative to come into and leave the soul, to move it with inspirations of love for His Divine Majesty. "With no previous occasion" means without any preceding awareness or knowledge of anything which might induce such comfort in the soul, by means of its own acts of intellect and will.

331. (3) Granted some occasion, a sense of comfort may be produced in the soul either by the good angel or the bad one, though with opposing ends in view. The good angel has in view the soul's progress, that it may grow by advancing from what is good to what is better. The evil spirit, contrariwise, tries to draw it to his own perverted designs and wickedness of will.

332. (4) It is typical of the evil spirit to transform himself into an angel of light, to go in by the devout soul's way but to come out his own way; I mean he introduces sound and pious thoughts, suited to the piety of that soul; but then, little by little, he tries to achieve his own purposes, by dragging the soul down to his secret designs and corrupt purposes.

333. (5) We should pay great attention to the entire train of thought. If beginning, middle and end are wholly sound, tending to what is completely innocent, this is a sign of the good angel; but the train of thought suggested sometimes leads to something that is bad or at least distracting, or less good than what the soul had originally proposed to do; sometimes it undermines our strength of mind or disturbs us by destroying our peace and tranquillity of mind and the unperturbed condition already obtaining: these are clear signs that the thoughts come from the evil spirit, the enemy of our progress and everlasting salvation.

334. (6) When the enemy of mankind is perceived and known by his serpent's tail, the evil conclusion to which he leads men, the person so tempted will find it useful afterwards to retrace the course of his thoughts, beginning with the good ideas originally suggested and the way in which he was gradually brought down from the heights of spiritual satisfaction and joy to accept the other's corrupt purpose. The understanding and noting of this experience will help him to be on his guard in future against the enemy's usual tricks.

335. (7) When souls are advancing from good to better, the touch of the good angel is soft, light and gentle, like a drop of water making its way into a sponge. The touch of the evil angel is rough, accompanied by noise and disturbance, like a drop of water falling on stone. But their action is the opposite with those who are going from bad to worse. The reason is that the state of soul is either contrary or similar to these angels. When it is contrary they make their way in with perceptible noise and sensation; when it is similar they come in quietly, like a man coming into his own house when the door is open.

336. (8) When the comfort has no preceding occasion, whilst it is true that this cannot be illusory, since it can come only from God our Lord, as we have said, yet the spiritual recipient must scrutinize the process with great care. He must distinguish exactly the specific time of the actual comforting from the subsequent stage when the soul is still glowing with the favour conferred on it, a sort of afterglow from the comforting which is now over. In this second stage the soul often makes different resolutions and plans which are not the direct result of the action of God our Lord. They may be due to the soul's own activity, based on established habits of mind or the implications of ideas or judgements previously formed; they may be the result of the action of the good or the evil spirit. So they have to be very carefully scrutinized before we can give them complete credit and put them into effect.

337. In the service of almsgiving the following rules should be kept.

338. (1) If I distribute anything to relatives, friends or persons to whom I feel an attachment, four considerations should be borne in mind. Some mention of them has been made in connection with the Decision.

The first is that the love whose influence prompts me to give alms is to be that which comes down from above, from the love of God our Lord, so that, from the outset, I am conscious that the degree of love I feel for these persons is for God's sake; in the motive moving me to greater love for them, the glory of God must be seen.

339. (2) I should imagine a man I have never seen or known, whose entire perfection I desire in the position and state of life he occupies. The norm I should wish him to adopt in his almsgiving, to the greater glory of God our Lord and the greater perfection of his own soul, is the norm I will adopt myself exactly, applying to my own case the rule and standard which I should wish for him, judging that to be what it should be.

340. (3) Picturing myself at the moment of death, I should ask myself what method and standard I shall then have wanted to maintain in my administrative duties. I shall regulate my life accordingly, and apply this standard to my almsgiving.

341. (4) Asking myself how I shall stand at the Day of Judgement, I will reflect carefully how I shall wish on that occasion to have acquitted myself of the duties and responsibilities of this office. I will now resolve to observe the rule I shall then wish to have kept.

342. (5) Thus, when a man feels moved by affection for certain individuals to whom he is anxious to give his property, he should pause and reflect carefully on the four rules given above, scrutinizing and testing his affection by them. Nor should he give any alms until he has eliminated and got rid of any irregularity in his attachment, according to these rules.

343. (6) There is, of course, no fault to be found with a man whose divine vocation it is to give alms if he receives the goods of God our Lord in order to distribute them. But there may well be question of erring by excess in estimating how much he ought to keep for himself out of the property he controls for distribution to others. He may therefore make use of the foregoing rules to reform his way of life and his standard of living.

344. (7) For the foregoing reasons and for many others, in anything that concerns his personal affairs and his standard of living, it is always safer and better for a man rather to limit himself, to cut down, and so draw nearer to our High Priest, our model and norm, Christ our Lord. This is in accordance with the resolution and decree of the Third Council of Carthage (attended by St Augustine), to the effect that a bishop's furniture should be cheap and poor. The same consideration should be applied to every state of life, due attention being paid to the condition and standing of the persons in question, and due proportion being observed. Thus, in matrimony, we have the example of St Joachim and St Anne, who divided their estate into three portions, giving one to the poor, one to the Temple ministry and service, keeping the third for the support of themselves and their family.

ABOUT SCRUPLES

345. THE following notes will help us to appreciate and understand the scruples and suggestions of our enemy.

346. (1) The name scruple is ordinarily given to an act of our own free choice and judgement by which we take for sin that which is not; for example, after treading accidentally on two crossed bits of straw, a man may conclude by his own judgement that he has sinned. But this is not strictly a scruple, being in fact an erroneous judgement.

347. (2) But suppose that, after treading on such a cross, or, it may be, after thinking or saying or doing something else, the idea occurs to me from outside myself that I have sinned, whilst on the other hand I do not think I have; however, I go on feeling this disturbance of mind, partly doubting and partly not doubting; this is properly a scruple and a temptation from the enemy.

348. (3) The first scruple referred to in the first note is wholly detestable, being downright error, but the next one referred to in the second note may, at least for a time, result in no small profit to the retreatant. It does in fact have a strong purifying and cleansing effect on such a soul, by going far to withdraw it from the mere semblance of sin. In St Gregory's words: *To see a fault where there is no fault is a sign of a well-disposed mind.*

349. (4) The enemy watches carefully to see if a soul is gross or sensitive. The sensitive he drives to the limit of sensitivity, the better to cause dismay and confusion. Thus, if he finds a soul that will not consent to any sin, mortal or venial, or even to what looks like sin, he recognizes that he will not be able to get it to fall into what has the appearance of sin. So he sets to work to persuade it to imagine that there is sin in something—a word or a passing thought—where there is no sin at all.

The gross conscience he tries to make even grosser. Thus, if formerly it made light of venial sins, he will now try to persuade it to regard mortal sins as unimportant. If formerly it had some hesitation about committing them he will try to diminish or eliminate such hesitation.

350. (5) The soul that is aiming at progress in the spiritual life must always adopt a procedure contrary to that of the enemy. If, that is, he tries to make it less sensitive, it must aim at a greater sensitivity of conscience; if he is trying to induce an excess of strictness, its efforts should be directed to finding perfect peace of mind on a sound basis of normal conduct.

351. (6) It may happen that the man in question wishes to express some view or perform some action within the framework of the Church's discipline and according to traditional opinion, which would be for the glory of God our Lord; the thought or, rather, temptation occurs to him from without not to speak or act in that way, specious arguments being adduced about vainglory or some such defect. He should then direct his attention to his Creator and Lord, and if he sees that his proposal is to God's due service or at least not against it, he should do what is the contrary of the temptation, recalling St Bernard's retort to the same tempter: "I did not start for you and I will not stop for you".

352. THE following rules are to be observed in order that we may hold the opinions we should hold in the Church militant.

353. (1) We should put away completely our own opinion and keep our minds ready and eager to give our entire obedience to our holy Mother the hierarchical Church, Christ our Lord's undoubted Spouse.

354. (2) We should speak with approval of confession to a priest, of the reception of Holy Communion once a year, still more once a month, most of all once a week, the requisite conditions being duly fulfilled.

355. (3) We should openly approve of the frequent hearing of Mass, and also of hymns, psalms and lengthy prayers both inside and outside the church, as well as the set times for the divine office as a whole, for prayer in general and for all the canonical hours.

356. (4) We should speak with particular approval of religious orders, and the states of virginity and celibacy, not rating matrimony as high as any of these.

357. (5) We should express approval of the vows of religion, poverty, obedience, and chastity, as well as of vows to perform other counsels of perfection. It is to be noted that a vow concerns activities conducive to the perfection of the Gospels; hence a vow should not be taken in matters far removed from those activities, such as going into business or getting married, and so on.

358. (6) We should approve of relics of the saints, showing reverence for them and praying to the saints themselves; visits to Station churches, pilgrimages, indulgences, jubilees, Crusade bulls, the lighting of candles in churches should all be commended.

359. (7) We should approve of the laws of fasting and abstinence in Lent, on Ember Days, vigils, Fridays and Saturdays, as well as mortifications both interior and exterior.

360. (8) We should praise church decoration and architecture, as well as statues, which we should venerate in view of what they portray.

361. (9) Finally, all the Church's commandments should be spoken of favourably, our minds being always eager to find arguments in her defence, never in criticism.

362. (10) We should be more inclined to approve and speak well of the regulations and instructions as well as the personal conduct of our superiors. It may well be that these are not or have not been always praiseworthy; but to criticize them, whether in public utterances or in dealing with ordinary people, is likely to give rise to complaint and scandal rather than to do good. This would arouse popular hostility towards authority both temporal and spiritual. Of course, whilst it does harm to speak ill of superiors behind their backs in the hearing of ordinary people, it can do good to point out their failings to these superiors themselves, who can correct them.

363. (11) Theology, both positive and scholastic, should be praised by us; on the one hand, the positive doctors, like St Jerome, St Augustine and St Gregory, have the special gift of moving men's hearts to a general love and service of God our Lord; the scholastics,

on the other hand, like St Thomas, St Bonaventure, the
Master of the Sentences and the rest, have their
special gift, which is rather to give precision to and
clarify, in a way suited to our age, those truths which
are necessary for eternal salvation. These scholastic
doctors, being nearer to our own times, not only have
the advantage of a correct understanding of the Sacred
Scriptures and of the positive doctors and saints but,
whilst being also enlightened and assisted themselves
by the power of God, they have the further assistance
of the Councils, Canons and decrees of our Holy
Mother the Church.

364. (12) We must be careful not to institute comparisons between our present generation and the saints
of former times, for this can be a source of great error.
We should not, for example, say: "He knows more
than St Augustine"; "He is another St Francis or even
greater"; "He is another St Paul in goodness, holiness",
etc.

365. (13) To arrive at complete certainty, this is the
attitude of mind we should maintain: I will believe
that the white object I see is black if that should be the
decision of the hierarchical Church, for I believe that
linking Christ our Lord the Bridegroom and His Bride
the Church, there is one and the same Spirit, ruling
and guiding us for our souls' good. For our Holy
Mother the Church is guided and ruled by the same
Spirit, the Lord who gave the Ten Commandments.

366. (14) Whilst it is absolutely true that no man
can be saved without being predestined and without
faith and grace, great care is called for in the way in
which we talk and argue about all these matters.

367. (15) Nor should we make a habit of talking about predestination. If we have to talk about it to some extent on occasion, our language should be such as not to lead ordinary people astray, as can happen if a man says: "It is already settled whether I am to be saved or damned; my good or bad conduct cannot make any difference". So they lose heart and cease to bother about the activities which make for their souls' health and spiritual profit.

368. (16) Again we must be careful lest, by over-much emphasis in talking about faith, without the necessary qualifications and clarifications, we give occasion to people to become indifferent and lazy about what they do, either before or after the acquisition of faith informed by charity.

369. (17) Nor should we talk so much about grace and with such insistence on it as to give rise to the poisonous view that destroys freedom. Thus, with the help of God, we should take every opportunity of talking about faith and grace, having in view the greater praise of His Divine Majesty; but our language and way of speaking should not be such that the value of our activities and the reality of human freedom might be in any way impaired or disregarded, especially in times like these which are full of dangers.

370. (18) It is of course true that we must esteem above all else the entire service of God out of sheer love; yet we should often speak in praise of the fear of His Divine Majesty. Not only is a childlike fear a good and holy attitude; so also is the fear proper to servants, which helps greatly to get men out of mortal sin when they are not capable of rising to the better and more effective form of love. Once they have got rid of mortal sin they can more easily rise to the child-like fear which is wholly acceptable and pleasing to God our Lord, since it is in accordance with His own love.